In love wit ...

Life of life

To Runa Mackay

In love with the
Life of life

Daily readings for Lent and Holy Week

Neil Paynter (ed)

wild goose
publications

www.ionabooks.com

First published 2020 by
Wild Goose Publications, 21 Carlton Court, Glasgow G5 9JP, UK,
the publishing division of the Iona Community.
Scottish Charity No. SC003794. Limited Company Reg. No. SC096243.

ISBN 978-1-84952-707-1

Overseas distribution
Australia: Willow Connection Pty Ltd, Unit 4A, 3–9 Kenneth Road,
Manly Vale, NSW 2093
New Zealand: Pleroma, Higginson Street, Otane 4170, Central Hawkes Bay
Canada: Bayard Distribution, 10 Lower Spadina Ave., Suite 400, Toronto,
Ontario M5V 2Z

Printed by Bell & Bain, Thornliebank, Glasgow

FSC
www.fsc.org
MIX
Paper from
responsible sources
FSC® C007785

Contents

Introduction

Someone once said to me that what they like about books like this one –
with so many contributors – is all the different voices. Reading collections
like this, they said, helped them to feel part of 'a little community of hope'.

In the book co-Leader of the Iona Community Kathy Galloway writes,
powerfully:

'… *It's about not living accommodated to a death-dealing world order. It's about
the choice to live. Life is what we have, life is the gift. I am in love with the Life
of life. So it's also a decision to live hopefully. And to be part of a community of
hope, with everyone who bears daily witness that the last word is the Life of
life, is to trust that in the embracing of the reality of death, there is a gift of
enormous agency, a power of love stronger than death, a possibility for transformation. And at the heart of our life as a community of love is gratitude, the
amazed wonder that it is indeed so, the 'being-in-love' that is a response to
experiencing the ground of our being as, beyond everything, grace.*'

I hope that reading this book helps you to feel part of a community of hope.
As 2020 dawns – we need hope.

Outside my window, daylight's coming up over the hills around Biggar. A
fragile winter light. But it won't be long until snowdrops are popping up
in our garden; daffodils unfurling in the pots out on the steps. Later, sun-
flowers might rise up out of thin earth like God.

I hope this book helps you to feel held within a community of hope, love,
gratitude, wonder, and that it challenges you to pray and work for the light
coming up over the hills of the world: folk working to fight climate change,
to welcome refugees and asylum seekers, to end poverty … Thank you so
much for what you do in your community and in the community of the
world. We are all sparks of the Light. Let's keep on encouraging and
inspiring each other.

To root this book and give writers a discipline, the Bible readings in the daily reading section are based on the Revised Common Lectionary, Year A. The Bible readings don't follow the lectionary strictly though: folk were asked to choose a few verses from one reading in the lectionary, and mostly did that. While the Bible readings connect to the lectionary for 2020, this book may be used any year in Lent. If you want to read it in connection with the lectionary it can be used every third year.

There is also a short section of general resources. This just naturally grew – I was sent so much rich and beautiful writing.

Reflecting a diverse community of hope, there's a good range of different writing styles here: biblical exegesis, personal reflection, meditation, poetry, prayer …

Thanks so much to everyone who contributed to *In love with the Life of life*, which was only started in the last part of 2019. It was a privilege to be entrusted with your writing.

Thanks to writer/editor/friend Ruth Burgess for her wise counsel and for being there.

As a new decade begins, let's say together:

We believe that God is present
in the darkness before dawn:
in the waiting and uncertainty
where fear and courage join hands,
conflict and caring link arms,
and the sun rises over barbed wire.

We believe in a with-us God,
who sits down in our midst
to share our humanity.

We affirm a faith
that takes us beyond the safe place:
into action, into vulnerability
and into the streets.

We commit ourselves to work for change
and put ourselves on the line;
to bear responsibility, take risks,
live powerfully and face humiliation;
to stand with those on the edge;
to choose life
and be used by the Spirit
for God's new community of hope.
Amen

– An Iona Community affirmation, from *Iona Abbey Worship Book*

Neil Paynter,
early January 2020,
Biggar, Scotland

Readings, prayers,
poems and actions
for Lent and Holy Week

First Week of Lent, Ash Wednesday

Bible readings: Isaiah 58:1–12; Psalm 51; 2 Corinthians 5:20b–6:10;
Matthew 6:1–6, 16–21

Call a public meeting.
Get everyone here.
Get them ready to listen and pray.
Make sure the old people come.
Bring the children, even the babies.
This is urgent.
Even contact those on their honeymoon.
Everyone needs to be here.

Tell them this:

Come back to God.
God is kind and full of mercy.
God is patient.
God keeps promises.
God is always ready to forgive.

Joel 2:13–16

Reflection:

Today is Ash Wednesday when many Christians gather to mark the beginning of Lent, traditionally a time of preparation for the mysteries of Holy
Week and Easter.

Some churches distribute ashes today, marking people with a cross on the
hand or the forehead, as a symbol of repentance and turning to God.

Ashes have also escaped outside the church. A movement called 'Ashes to
Go' marks Ash Wednesday in places where people gather – in shopping
centres, at markets and railway stations, outside courthouses, on city

streets. People going about their daily lives are offered the opportunity to receive ashes, and to think about God's love for them and for the world. This is not a movement that aims to replace services in churches, rather to share liturgy in public places.

Christian CND and Pax Christi often join together for a service on Ash Wednesday outside the Ministry of Defence in London and at other places. Their liturgy includes prayers for repentance for the UK's continued possession of nuclear weapons, and they often use sackcloth and ashes as powerful symbols.

A reflection on fasting:

Fasting?
OK, God,
first thoughts:
sackcloth and ashes.
Giving up something … smoking … chocolate … booze?
Trying to be extra kind instead of giving something up?
Images of you as angry and wanting us to feel miserable –
of you as not being very nice!

So, the day's lectionary readings:
well, Matthew seems to be saying
whatever we do on the fasting front
we need to do it secretly and quietly,
and that prayer,
spending time talking with you
and listening to you,
is part of the picture.

The psalmist is definitely into a heavy
sin and guilt trip
but he does ask you for wisdom
and knows that you look for integrity and truth in our lives.

Paul tells us
that today is the day to act,
rather than tomorrow

And then there's Isaiah,
who has some very clear ideas as to what fasting is about:
to take burdens off people,
to work for justice,
to share food with those who are hungry,
to share hospitality,
to give clothes to those who need them.

So how am I going to keep Lent?
By praying?
By sharing food and hospitality?
By being active in organisations and movements that seek justice?
By keeping what I'm doing, or not doing, a secret?
By thinking and reading and experiencing what you're really about?

It's Ash Wednesday.
Time for fasting.
Time to turn away from the bad stuff.
Time to turn to God.

Prayer:

From dust we come,
to dust we will return:
we belong to God.

Bless us now at the beginning of Lent;
hear our regrets, our prayers, our dreams.
Keep us close to you, God.
Keep us close to you.
Amen

Actions:

— Can you find somewhere you can receive ashes today?

— Read about the Ashes to Go movement (https://ashestogo.org). Could you offer something like this in your community next year?

— Light a small fire of paper or wood and watch it as it burns into ashes and dust.

Ruth Burgess

First Week of Lent, Thursday

Bible reading:

The word of the Lord came to Jonah a second time, saying, 'Get up, go to Nineveh, that great city, and proclaim to it the message that I tell you.'

Jonah 3:1 (NRSV)

Reflection:

The Book of Jonah is a strange story which is full of great adventure. God sends Jonah on a mission to the city of Nineveh but Jonah takes a ship in the opposite direction. A fearful storm arises, and the sailors blame Jonah. They throw Jonah overboard, and he is swallowed by a great fish. Jonah sits desolate in the belly of the fish for three days. During this time he prays earnestly to God for help. Then he is spewed out from the fish onto dry land. At the start of our reading the word of God comes to Jonah for 'a second time', and this time he does go to Nineveh. In a three-day walk across the city, he calls the people to repent. Jonah 3 describes the miraculous repentance of all the inhabitants. They proclaim a fast and put on sackcloth. The king takes off his robe, puts on sackcloth, and sits in ashes.

The sudden repentance of the city of Nineveh is astounding, and it points to the possibility of change. It seems incredible but we can think of great historical changes that almost took us by surprise – the fall of the Berlin Wall – the end of apartheid in South Africa and the creation of the Truth and Reconciliation Commission – the Good Friday Agreement. These historical changes are turning points in which years of tension and enmity are overcome. At these times we are able to catch sight of a new possibility of peace and freedom in the world. For years change has seemed impossible, but underneath the surface of life the Spirit has been moving. Many unseen people have been working for peace and freedom; people who have remained committed in times of injustice and persecution.

In our reading, Jonah is commanded to speak the word of God but he is a reluctant prophet. He does not want the people of Nineveh to repent. Jonah is angry at their evil ways and their violence. He knows that God is merciful, but he does not want God to forgive the people of Nineveh. Yet the prophetic word does not go unheard. The repentance of the people of Nineveh is a challenge to Jonah.

At the end of the book, Jonah also needs to undergo a change of heart, for he has no compassion. Jonah sits outside the city in the heat. God gives him a bush for shade but the next day God sends a worm to attack the bush and it withers. Jonah is very angry about the loss of the bush – but God asks Jonah why he is more concerned about the bush than the people and animals of the city. Jonah is confronted with the truth that God cares for all people.

Today many people are concerned about climate change, the suffering of asylum seekers and refugees and the growing divide between the rich and poor – great changes are needed in our society on many levels. The story of Jonah reminds us that wholehearted change is possible – even in the places of oppression in our world. The story is also concerned with the importance of reconciliation on a personal level. In some of the great turning points in our society, we see people setting aside the conflicts of the past to seek peace in the present. The story of Jonah is a challenge to us to look into our own hearts and to seek mercy not judgement on our opponents, to help build a new world of peace and freedom.

Prayer:

God of freedom and peace,
help us to hear your prophetic word,
even when it takes us to places
where we do not want to go.
Keep us faithful and give us courage.
When we sit desolate in the belly of the great fish
help us to challenge the powerful
and to see that change is possible
in our world and in ourselves.
Give us hearts of mercy and compassion.
Amen

Susan Miller

First Week of Lent, Friday

Bible reading:

... God said to Jonah, 'Is it right for you to be angry about the bush? ... for which you did not labour and which you did not grow; it came into being in a night and perished in a night. And should I not be concerned about Nineveh, that great city, in which there are more than a hundred and twenty thousand persons who do not know their right hand from their left, and also many animals?'

Jonah 4:9–11 (NRSV)

Reflection: 'What is God thinking?'

The Book of Jonah would make a great cartoon or graphic novel. Cartoons often put a thought bubble above a character's head. I see Jonah heading off for Tarshish, rejecting his first commission from God to preach repentance in Nineveh, wearing a thought bubble that reads 'What is God thinking?' No way is Jonah signing on to God's plan to invite those wicked Ninevites to change their tune. Better God should wipe them off the face of the earth!

A few days later, when Jonah considers his plight in the belly of the great fish, that thought bubble might read 'What was I thinking?' His prayer from the depths reaches out to God for mercy, promising more grateful sacrifices if only God will rescue Jonah.

But Jonah should have known better. No sooner has that cartoon fish spit Jonah out than God renews the challenge: 'Proclaim repentance to Nineveh!' We watch the reluctant prophet trudge through the streets of that large city, shouting half-heartedly, 'Forty days more, and Nineveh shall be overthrown.' The thought bubble reappears: 'Forty days more? What is God thinking?' Too much time, in Jonah's opinion. And sure enough, the inhabitants of Nineveh repent. From patriarch to pet cat, they put on sackcloth and observe a fast, hoping God will also repent from anger that would destroy them.

As today's reading begins, Jonah's thought bubble bursts. He shouts out to God in prayer: 'What were you thinking? I just knew you'd be merciful to this city of no-good Ninevites. You are so full of steadfast love, it makes me sick!' We watch as Jonah stomps out of the city in righteous anger. God calls out, 'Is it right for you to be so angry?' I hear God's voice filled with some pain, and a plea for Jonah himself to turn from his anger. How can Jonah fail to understand? Anger is so destructive.

The final scene pictures Jonah with a bush which flourishes quickly 'to save him from his discomfort'. At first we see Jonah smile, pleased with God's kindness. But in the morning, this animated plant withers; the unrelenting cartoon sun beats down on Jonah's head, and the sultry wind bakes the prophet himself. 'What was God thinking?' Jonah sulks. 'It is better for me to die.'

Finally Jonah must learn what God has been thinking all along. God argues that Jonah feels more compassion for a bush, here today and gone tomorrow, than a hundred and twenty thousand souls in Nineveh – plus their animals. God is thinking that Jonah has his priorities mixed up. God is thinking that mercy is more powerful than sin or grievance over sin. God is thinking that Jonah himself needs to embrace repentance and let go of his anger.

The challenge for any animated version of Jonah's story is the ending. This standoff between God and the pouting prophet remains unresolved. What is Jonah thinking now? In the remaining tension lies the opportunity for Lenten reflection. Are we tempted to withhold the invitation of God's mercy to those whom we find undeserving? This is a common reaction when we feel wronged by an individual. But the fact that ancient Nineveh was located in modern-day Iraq expands our reflections. These days popular sentiment readily turns against nations in conflict with our own, or migrants from cultures different from our own. In today's geopolitics, appeals for mercy toward those regarded as threats are drown out by fear and anger. God's response to Jonah provokes our prayers for a world in which overheated anger threatens justice for the vulnerable and peace among neighbours and nations. The Book of Jonah reminds us that God is always thinking about mercy and the possibilities for the renewed life it creates. Let us pray that neighbours and nations alike will repent of anger towards those they consider enemies and remember God's merciful heart.

Prayer:

God of mercy, in your presence,
we confess those times
when we have cherished anger toward people and places
which somehow gave us offence.
Forgive us our own hardness of heart
which leads us to give up on the power of mercy
to create new beginnings.
In these times when distrust and anger
colour the world stage and deepen divisions,
we pray that you will call neighbours and nations
to repent of their anger
and turn from dangerous, divisive action.
Inspire us to trust in your mercy and seek
to live it out in our own relationships and attitudes
for the sake of Christ,
Mercy Incarnate.
Amen

Nancy Cocks

First Week of Lent, Saturday

Bible reading:

… The disciples came to Jesus and asked, 'Who is the greatest in the kingdom of heaven?' He called a child, whom he put among them, and said, 'Truly I tell you, unless you change and become like children, you will never enter the kingdom of heaven. Whoever becomes humble like this child is the greatest in the kingdom of heaven.'

Matthew 18:1–4 (NRSV)

Reflection: No joke

If you read this book in its year of publication, Day 4 of Lent would be 29th February 2020, and Jesus teaching about becoming like children would coincide with my friend Joan's twenty-second birthday celebration.

Twenty-two years of age may not be the best example of childhood. In fact, there are those amongst us with no sense of humour who insist her age in 2020 would be eighty-eight. They say she became twenty-two in 1954. By Joan's reckoning, however, in 1954 she was only five and a half!

I know quite a few people who would love to reclaim their youth. I might be one of them. I don't know anyone else who does it Joan's way though. Few have the opportunity. It is an accident of birth.

Joan is only joking, of course. So am I, in comparing her leap-year joke with the words of Jesus.

But Jesus wasn't joking. When he told his friends to become like children, he meant it. He had caught them competing for the highest places before. This time they might have just been checking that the same intolerant officials wouldn't be in control for all eternity. Well, Jesus made it clear. 'Forget hierarchy!' he said. 'My kingdom is nothing to do with who's in charge. It's for the powerless, the voiceless, the marginalised and forgotten. If you want to be part of it, change your ideas and become like children. Let's have some humility here!'

Not that he thought of children as humble. Or wanted them to be. He liked them as they were. He blessed them; enjoyed their singing and playing and quarrelling; even beckoned one of them over to make his point.

What's more, the child came: stood there in the middle of a group of grown-ups. Children trusted him like that. They would happily dance along with a palm-waving crowd for him; follow him into the temple, shouting at the top of their voices to the annoyance of the men in charge. They knew Jesus wouldn't mind. He did some pretty outrageous things in the temple himself. He was OK, was Jesus.

No, Jesus wasn't joking. He wasn't joking when he said what he said about people who broke the trust of children. He might have exaggerated a bit with his comments about anvils and oceans, because adults who abused the young made him very angry. But joking he was not. He loved children. He wanted a kingdom full of them. Children of five and a half and less. Children of eighty-eight and more.

Prayer:

You say we must be like children, Lord;
yet you don't want us to be childish.
So what do you mean exactly?
You talk in riddles. You tell us parables.
Your teaching is so important,
yet you leave us to work it out.
Why?

That's what children do, isn't it?
They ask 'Why?'
Why this? Why that? Questions, questions.
They're just starting out; they want to know everything;
they want to test us out.

For them it's all in the future.
Such innocence!

… Though I sometimes wonder whether they are really that innocent.
Perhaps it is that they just haven't been tamed yet.
They haven't been told what to think.
They are still allowed to dream. And daydream.
They live off imagination and hope;
come up with fantastic ideas; draw amazing pictures.
They try things out, and when they make mistakes, they laugh.

Well, it comes to the same thing as innocence –
they are dangerously open.
Is that the sort of people you want in your kingdom –
adults that behave like that?

Then tell me this, Lord:
could it be that you are actually asking us to learn from them –
from their hopes and dreams and impractical ideas?
Are you suggesting they should be our teachers?
Like the prophet said? 'A little child shall lead them'?
Really?

Well, I've just remembered something, from years back,
when our daughters were little.
I was trying to work something out, something geographical,
and my atlas didn't give me the information I wanted.
I needed the globe that was in their bedroom;
so I tiptoed in and found it.
But as I was carrying it to the door, a voice came from the bedclothes:
'What are you doing with my world?'

Did you hear that question too, Lord?
It has haunted me ever since.
Now, they are all asking it:
asking it of us!

Suddenly I want to stand with them –
because all their imagination, all their dreams and amazing pictures –
they don't only come packaged in laughter, do they?
There's fear there too; there's sadness and anger.
It's their future, isn't it!
We thought we were guiding them, protecting them, taming them,
but they really are our teachers, Lord!

So are these the kind of children you want us all to be? –
children who ask 'Why?' with placards and politics,
and make peace as well as promises;
and who, if they pray 'Your kingdom come',
are seeking a future for earth as well as a life in heaven?

I am asking you, Lord. I'm asking many questions,
because I no longer know all the answers.
I'm asking like a child.

Brian Woodcock

First Sunday of Lent

Bible reading:

Then Jesus was led up by the Spirit into the wilderness to be tempted by the devil. He fasted for forty days and forty nights, and afterwards he was famished. The tempter came and said to him, 'If you are the Son of God, command these stones to become loaves of bread.'

... Again, the devil took him to a very high mountain and showed him all the kingdoms of the world and their splendour, and he said to him: 'All these I will give you, if you will fall down and worship me.' Jesus said to him, 'Away with you, Satan! For it is written,

"Worship the Lord your God,
  and serve only him."'

Then the devil left him, and suddenly angels came and waited on him.

Matthew 4:1–3, 8–11 (NRSV)

Reflection:

The desert ...... endless space and harsh light. Vast skies of wheeling stars. Oranges yellows pinks purples of sun rising and setting. The endless hours between the first light and the fading colours of evening. Dry earth, rock, the wadi. Birds circling. Lizards scuttle. A trail of ants crosses the red earth. A flash of green. Solitary bush. No shelter there.

Hunger comes and goes. Gnawing. Hard to walk now. Pounding head in the sunlight. And such a dry mouth in this bleached parched land. Empty. No fresh drip drip drip of water. No deep clear pool. No spring gushing out from the dry riverbed.

No softness. No tender growth. No human hand to touch.

So alone now. All these hours and days. Reality is the fierce sun burning and consuming my being. Reality is God burning and consuming my being.

The endless light which holds me.

Doubts twist me. Why this, why now? So little time left to reach them all. Such a lost world while I navel-gaze here. No time for self-indulgent spiritual exercises. And what have I done? What difference have I made? With so much need all around.

Some bread just to strengthen me. Soft freshly baked bread warm from the oven. Famished. The scent of ripe figs. A cup of wine from the village. Strength returning. Vitality flowing back. The joy of movement. Walking back to my people. To go out and act. To do what's needed.

Or a sign. Something clear and emphatic, leaving no space for doubt. To save them, and help them to see the truth. Not this endless ineffectual muddle of people and demands and mess. There isn't time for all of this – the smallness of life, the slow misunderstood journeys. I can reach so few of them. And it takes so long. One clear message to show God's power. And then things can change and move, then the walls tumble and the doubts vanish.

And the powerful – how to reach them? How to show God's truth to the world? To Jerusalem? To Rome? Enough power to fix it all. An unambiguous message – God is in charge here. All that richness and glory put to God's use. And the dreams of what could be done ...... Power used to transform worlds. Power in my hands, safe hands. Enemies, the haters, brought low. Armies overwhelmed. The world convinced. One ruler, one truth, my life finding its true purpose. No more fear; no more loneliness; no more doubt.

Dazzling dreams and images. Long hours filled with the absence of the presence of God. The lure of possibilities, of different realities. Visions shimmering in the midday sun. Bread. Clarity. Power. The lack of ambiguity. The seductive path.

The rocks bruise my feet. The sun scorches my skin. The night wind chills and moans.

Then a freshening air. The soft grey light before dawn. Tiny yellow flowers in a crack in the rock. A bird soaring in the blue. The scent of water ...

And a brush of wings. A rush of air. Stillness. Held in loving arms.

The simplicity and the enormity of the task.

A clear path through the wilderness to what lies ahead.

Prayer:

Jesus of the desert ways,
walk with us as we leave comforting truths
familiar certainties
and travel with you into the silence and empty spaces of the wilderness.
Strengthen us to live, stripped of illusions, with you:
Confronting ourselves and our demons and angels.
Resisting the glitter of easy answers.
Staying with you in our fear and doubt.
So that we may share your journey towards Easter morning.

Christian MacLean

Second Week of Lent, Monday

Bible reading:

Happy are those whose transgression is forgiven,
whose sin is covered …

… I acknowledged my sin to you,
*　and I did not hide my iniquity;*
I said 'I will confess my transgressions to the Lord',
*　and you forgave the guilt of my sin.*

Psalm 32:1,5 (NRSV)

Reflection:

When I was discussing guilt with my daughter Claire, she said, 'The trouble with guilt is that you tend to ruminate upon it.' And that can be so very true. If we spend too much time feeling guilty then that guilt can take the joy out of life.

Jesus brought the power of Old Testament writings to his message: 'Love God and your neighbour as yourself.' It is all too easy to think of that verse as simply 'Love God and your neighbour', and not to think about the ending 'as yourself'. Do we love ourselves? Is it easier to forgive our neighbours than ourselves? We, after all, must live with what we have done. But we need to be able to free ourselves from disabling feelings, as the psalmist has done, if we are to live lives full of love, kindness and compassion.

A story is told of U.S. President Garfield, who was encouraged to take a profitable but slightly dishonest course of action. He was reassured, 'No one will ever know.' And he replied, 'But President Garfield will know, and I have to sleep with him tonight.'

We all feel guilty about things that have happened. Jesus taught: 'I have come that you may have life, and have it abundantly' (Jn 10:10), and that requires of us, among many things, forgiveness, not just of others but also of self, perhaps especially of self.

Jesus said: 'The Kingdom of God is within you' (Lk 17:21). Can that be true? Is the Kingdom of God that Jesus spoke about an inner condition of loving-kindness and compassion – both for our neighbours and ourselves? The key to moving on from our guilt may be forgiveness, and being kind and compassionate to ourselves, and trying never to repeat the action that caused the guilt.

Robert Burns, experiencing guilt and depression for many of his actions, wrote:

Oh!, enviable, early days,
When dancing thoughtless pleasure's maze,
To care, to guilt unknown!
How ill exchang'd for riper times,
To feel the follies, or the crimes,
Of others, or my own!

(From 'Despondency')

The Psalmist has acknowledged personal sin, confessed it and speaks confidently about that guilt being forgiven. Doing the same may allow us to move on, to live our lives abundantly, full of compassion, love and kindness.

Prayer:

Lord, help me to confess my sins to you,
always seeking your forgiveness.
Help me to understand why I committed these sins
and strengthen my desire not to repeat them.
Help me to develop a spirit of forgiveness for others
and also for myself.
Please also help me live a life full of compassion, love and kindness,
this Lent and always.
Amen

Allan Gordon

Second Week of Lent, Tuesday

Bible reading:

'Since, then, we have a great high priest who has passed through the heavens, Jesus, the Son of God, let us hold fast to our confession. For we do not have a high priest who is unable to sympathise with our weaknesses, but we have one who in every respect has been tested as we are, yet without sin. Let us therefore approach the throne of grace with boldness, so that we may receive mercy and find grace to help in time of need.'

Hebrews 4:14–16 (NRSV)

Reflection:

For some who open the pages of this book, the notion of priesthood belongs to the clerical role: a specially called, distinctively set-apart person. We may know women and men who live their ordained priesthood with integrity and whose gravitas resonates within people's humanity and influences for good all sorts and conditions.

Hopefully we also have grown to recognise the inner priestliness of every human being, the indwelling of the divine within all persons. It is within the depths of our humanity that the divine fertility abides, awakening awareness, possibility, promise, curiosity, imagination, our inner longings, calling forth and realising our coming into being. It is within the complexity of daily life that grace and truth are embodied. This is the divine 'calling forth' within all persons, the inner priestliness. On this holy ground we take our shoes off!

The verses we have been given to meditate on present us with a paradox. Jesus, our great high priest, sympathises with our weaknesses and in every respect was tested as we are, 'yet without sin'. Alongside this we live with the Jesus who was 'numbered with the transgressors' (Is 53:12); who consented to enter the waters of baptism alongside those who repented of their sins (Lk 3:3); who died between two criminals (Lk 23:32); and who, in Paul's words,

'For our sake he made him to be sin who knew no sin …' (2 Cor 5:21). We may understandably continue to ponder what this might mean for us.

A few years ago I saw the trailer for the BBC series *Broken* but chose not to watch – however in the weeks that followed friends persuaded me of the programme's value. In my judgement it is a remarkable and courageous piece of television. The drama tells of a Catholic priest among the people in the deprived community he serves in a northern city, a broken priest among people who are broken, in a broken society. It is compassionate, thoughtful and tough. The flawed priest, Father Michael, thinks he has failed the people, but they know he has served them well.

Prayer:

Lord, in your mercy,
transform us.

Donald Eadie

Second Week of Lent, Wednesday

Bible reading:

'What do you think? If a shepherd has a hundred sheep, and one of them has gone astray, does he not leave the ninety-nine on the mountains and go in search of the one that went astray? And if he finds it, truly I tell you, he rejoices over it more than over the ninety-nine that never went astray.'

Matthew 18:12–13 (NRSV)

Reflection:

It is an old image: the king as shepherd who protects his flock. Even the pharaoh Ramses used it more than 3000 years ago to tell his subjects that he was there to take care of his people and watch over them.

The image was popular and easily understandable. It is a favourite both in the Hebrew Bible and in the New Testament. 'The Lord is my shepherd' we pray with countless people who have regularly prayed these wonderful words of vision and comfort.

An old image. But is it really the image of the pharaoh? The king made God? Or rather: God made human? What is special about the shepherd of the New Testament parables? For me it is the passionate, almost provocative, search for the one sheep who has gone astray. How can a shepherd abandon all his flock, only to search for one wayward animal?! Still, the way Jesus asks – 'if a shepherd has a hundred sheep, and one of them has gone astray, does he not leave the ninety-nine and go in search of the one?' – suggests that all shepherds would do the same.

There is no criticism, neither of the shepherd nor of the lost sheep. Maybe the animal was weak from the very start, maybe it was sick, had fallen on the rocky ground and hurt itself? There are so many reasons for getting lost. Bad reasons but also good ones. Sometimes I get lost because something is so beautiful and intriguing that I need to have a closer look – only a moment it seems, but then the flock has already passed on by.

The good shepherd of the Bible cares for each and every sheep, especially those in need of help.

Now, however, this parable is told in the context of saving the sinner. The lost sheep is being sought (the father welcomes home the prodigal son, the woman who lost one drachma searches her whole house). And everywhere there is rejoicing when what was lost is found.

I have always sympathised with the ninety-nine sheep that did what was expected of them – and with that frustrated elder brother who had never stopped labouring for his father.

How come I've put myself so easily on the side of the 'good'?

Maybe the good are not the good after all?

Maybe they are the sinners who never dared and never cared and simply trotted one after the other! Maybe obedience is a compromised virtue that always begs the question: who is at the centre of your attention and obedience? …

Who do I follow?

I want to be an apprentice of the good shepherd.
I want to learn when to go after the lost sheep,
and when to stay put and let them find their way;
when to protect and comfort,
and when to challenge.

I want to be your apprentice, Jesus,
and learn from you
when to fight
and when to surrender into
the everlasting arms of love …

Who is following me?
Who do I follow?

Who do you follow?

Reinhild Traitler-Espiritu

Second Week of Lent, Thursday

Bible reading:

Listen to me, you that pursue righteousness,
*   you that seek the Lord.*
Look to the rock from which you were hewn,
*   and to the quarry from which you were dug.*

Isaiah 51:1 (NRSV)

Reflection:

Steven Spielberg's film *Amistad* shows how the U.S. Supreme Court in 1845 ruled that Africans who had liberated themselves from a Spanish slave ship should be returned home, rather than returned to their captors. The day before the judgement, the lawyer and former President John Quincy Adams warned the leader of the captives, Cinque, that they had little chance of winning their freedom. 'But we will not be going in (to the Court) alone,' said Cinque. 'Indeed no,' replied Adams. 'We have right and righteousness on our side.' Cinque smiled, but offered a different angle. 'Last night,' he said, 'I summoned my ancestors from the beginning of time and begged them to help us. They must come. I am the whole reason they have existed.'

Western theologians and some missionaries have often looked down on what they have erroneously called 'ancestor worship'. But the people of the Bible were much more tuned to these sacred connections. When Jesus took his disciples Peter, James and John up a mountain, they had a vision of their master talking with two of Israel's great ancestors – Moses and Elijah. The Hebrew people in the Old Testament were constantly reminded by the prophets of their particular heritage as the 'people of God'. It was a sacred trust and that laid special obligations on them.

Of course we can easily romanticise (and distort) our heritage. In Scotland we overplay our traditional love of freedom in church and state, forgetting that religion has been too often used as a means of control, and that Scots have played a major role in the enslavement of others in the Empire.

History and heritage is never clear cut. Because one third of the petitions of ordinary people against the British slave trade came from Scotland, and many Scots, such as Zachary Macaulay from a Highland manse, were key figures with William Wilberforce in the movement for the abolition movement of chattel slavery.

A constant reminder threaded through the Old Testament was 'Do not oppress the alien or the foreigner. Remember that you yourself were foreigners and slaves in Egypt, and the Lord delivered you.' But we do forget. The strictly religious Afrikaners, having suffered in British concentration camps in the early 20th century, went on to devise the oppressive system of Apartheid in South Africa and imposed it on those who were classified as 'non-whites'. The modern state of Israel, half a century after those camps in South Africa, gave shelter to victims of long-standing racial persecution and survivors of the Holocaust. Ironically that same state quickly transformed into a modern-day example of ethnic cleansing at the expense of the Palestinian people.

How do we acknowledge our debt to the rocks from which we were hewn in the past, and not be bound by them? Perhaps the clue is in Isaiah's injunction to seek the 'righteousness' of God. Karen Armstrong, a leading writer on religion, claims that the litmus test for any authentic religion is compassion. Certainly the gospels show that to be a clear priority in the teaching and ministry of Jesus. One of his elderly contemporaries, Rabbi Hillel of Jerusalem, was once laughed at by a sceptic, who said he would become a believer if the Rabbi could teach him the whole of the Torah while standing on one leg. The old man came to his feet and balanced shakily. 'Whatever is harmful to you,' he said, 'do not do to another. That is the Torah. All else is commentary.'

John Quincy Adams, in *Amistad,* pointed the judges to the Founding Fathers of the nation, and urged them not to take lightly their influence or heritage. 'Who we are,' he declared, 'is who we were.' He was not naive enough to ignore the stark truth that the very institution of slavery was at odds with the professed ideals of the new nation. But in that stylised drama of the case, we can see clearly that in every generation we need to take fresh stock of the rocks from which we were hewn, and where we stand in the light of God's righteousness.

Prayer:

God of the ages,
you link us with our ancestors:
those we have heard stories about,
the adventurers and the explorers,
the campaigners,
those who were killed in pointless wars;
the remembered and the long-forgotten.
You link us with our loved ones, who nurtured
and guided, encouraged and cried over us –
gone from us, but present in our genes, our hearts, our souls –
the foundations, the cornerstones.
The walls, roofs, open doors.

God of faithfulness, of hopefulness,
we would be the foundation stones for future generations,
yet we lack the courage, the faith and even the cheerfulness.
Strengthen us. Give us courage to heal the failing world,
to scatter the stones and to gather them for future generations.
Amen

Iain & Isabel Whyte

Second Week of Lent, Friday

Bible reading:

I lift up my eyes to the hills –
   from where will my help come?
My help comes from the Lord,
   who made heaven and earth.

Psalm 121:1–2 (NRSV)

Reflection:

As you look up and out, what do you see today? Do the walls of your home form the boundaries of your setting? Do office blocks, shops and houses sculpt an urban backdrop for your activities? Or is the horizon more open with coast and sea? Does it unfold in hill, river, forest or field?

Each one of us is living and moving through a particular landscape: urban or rural, comforting or challenging, mundane or exciting. We may have great purpose as we go or we may simply be carried along within the usual framework and rhythm of our days. Either way, we are all travellers, pilgrims even, as we navigate the path before us.

So, just now, as you look up, what do you see? Dare to consider what is before you in all its fullness.

The flattest and calmest sea can stir to violent storm which surges and engulfs all before it. The highest buildings can offer us breathtaking and expansive views from above whilst enclosing and confining those below. The refuge and safety of home may yet isolate and hold captive. The forest can provide shelter but may also disorient and leave us lost.

The hills drew the gaze of the psalmist journeying to Jerusalem. The hills filled the way ahead with their splendour and yet there was the potential for threat and challenge on their heights; they had to be overcome. The psalmist looked and the hills spoke; they drew forth the question: from where will my help come?

The psalmist looked and the hills also answered. They declared the majesty and the creativity of God. Help would come from the maker of heaven and earth.

The psalmist's posture and intent capture my attention. The eyes were lifted so the head was up. There was a deliberate and thoughtful attentiveness to the way ahead and to the question that was being stirred within as the psalmist considered that road; a question that was not suppressed but given voice; a question which left space for an answer; an answer which ultimately declared and expressed faith in God.

Yet we may hesitate to lift our eyes for there may be challenges ahead and ones that feel too great to face full on.

When the seas roar and foam and we look up, though, we might see Jesus walking across the waves towards us speaking his presence and peace to us; stilling the storm within us.

When the noise and pace of the city, the demands and challenges of work engulf us and we look up, we may see Jesus inviting us, weary as we are, to come to him and find rest.

When we are hemmed in by our circumstances and the road seems impossible to travel and we look up, we may find strength and courage as we see Jesus acknowledging that in this world we will have trouble and yet encouraging us to take heart for he has overcome the world.

When we cannot see the woods for the trees, when we look around and nothing feels safe or familiar and we look up, we may see Jesus reminding us that he is with us always and inviting us to follow him.

When we lie in green pastures by still waters and we look up, we may see the Good Shepherd watching over us and prayers of praise and thanksgiving may overflow in us to the maker of heaven and earth.

Action:

On this Lenten journey, the invitation today is to look up at the way ahead of you; to lift your eyes and be attentive to what you see. Befriend what stirs within you. Give it voice in prayer. If it is a question, be attentive today, and in the days to come, for an answer.

Sarah Dickinson

Second Week of Lent, Saturday

Bible reading:

After Jesus had finished all his sayings in the hearing of the people, he entered Capernaum. A centurion there had a slave whom he valued highly, and who was ill and close to death. When he heard about Jesus, he sent some Jewish elders to him, asking him to come and heal his slave. When they came to Jesus, they appealed to him earnestly, saying, 'He is worthy of having you do this for him, for he loves our people, and it is he who built our synagogue for us.' And Jesus went with them, but when he was not far from the house, the centurion sent friends to say to him, 'Lord, do not trouble yourself, for I am not worthy to have you come under my roof; therefore I did not presume to come to you. But only speak the word, and let my servant be healed …'

When Jesus heard this he was amazed at him, and turning to the crowd that followed him, he said, 'I tell you, not even in Israel have I found such faith.' When those who had been sent returned to the house, they found the slave in good health.

Luke 7:1–7, 9–10 (NRSV)

Reflection:

This challenging story is also found in Matthew's Gospel. Every line in it is full of rich humanity. A dimension of genuine caring threads through. It is an important passage in these weeks before Easter as we seek developments and growth within our own faith in Christ. This passage weaves together expectancy, awareness of guilt, compassion, belief and healing. All these have been dimensions in the Lent liturgies since the days of the early church; they are also deep in the fabric of Celtic worship. Perhaps the story has more meaning for me now, living with an incurable cancer, then it did previously. Even if my myeloma is not at present curable, like the slave in our story, I too seek God's healing in body, mind and spirit.

The passage makes it clear that the centurion is an honourable person and his friends remind Jesus of the good things he has done for the whole of the local community. Jesus responds to their request and sets out to visit his house but on the way there the officer sends a message which is both simple and honest: 'I am not worthy to meet you in person and there is no need to come to my place, but if you just say the word, my servant will be healed.' As a military person he was used to orders, both giving and receiving them.

Jesus was surprised when he heard this message, and told the folk following him that he had never found faith like this, even in Israel.

It's not difficult to understand why he was amazed. In any century, faith in God has many twists and turns. Days of sure belief may be followed by days of equally strong doubt. These mixed convictions and doubts are for me embedded in our spiritual DNA and they make all of us to some degree unpredictable. Jesus understands this well, but also instantly recognised on that Capernaum street that his word of love and the servant's level of expectancy would bring healing. It did. The slave returned, as scripture tells us, 'to good health'.

In reflecting upon this particular passage, I am encouraged by a truth within my own faith journey. It is this: Yes, there may be days, even years, of doubt about our belief in God, but sometimes, and usually without much warning, we are touched deep in our souls by the reality of the Holy Spirit.

In Lent may we take time each day to be still and quiet: to come to realise that the Spirit surrounds us, enfolds us just as we are, in our strengths and weaknesses.

I tried to express this in a prayer many years ago:

Knowing, yet unknown,
without a name, yet holding every name,

often unexpectantly you come close,
and in tenderness reveal
the meaning of our lives
and the pattern of our days.

Today may I sit for a moment without words
and experience your light.

Peter Millar

Second Sunday of Lent

Bible reading:

I look at the mountains;
where will my help come from?
My help will come from God the Maker,
who will not let me fall and is always awake.

From Psalm 121 (my own remembered version)

Reflection:

Did you know that Psalm 121 is called 'the traveller's psalm'? I didn't until I walked the 'End to End' (from one end of Britain to the other) in the spring and summer of 2019, in 117 days. Benedictines, like myself, are particularly attached to the Psalms, and I would often use my remembered Psalter during the day as I walked, and in the evenings as I rested.

Day 59 was in Cumbria – and there are plenty of mountains and hills there – so Psalm 121 was ideal. The walk began earlier than usual. We decided on an early start because the forecast was for heavy rain arriving from lunchtime onwards. With 8 miles to walk in the day, I got started at Carlingill Bridge at 8am. The route followed the valley through which the M6 and the West Coast Main Line also travels but I was on the back road.

Near High Carlingill Farm an intriguing notice said that the site was being excavated as part of the *Digging for Britain* TV series. The route was along a Roman road; there was the site of a Roman fort nearby. But at this other site there was evidence of the pre-Roman British inhabitants. I look forward to the programme. People have lived in these hills for a long long time and, in the same way as the Psalmist, probably looked up at them and prayed and wondered.

At Salterwath Bridge (the name indicates an old salt route) I took the path by the River Lune through woodland and farmland. I met Bob, my husband, on this section and we emerged onto the road at Lune Bridge. We had early elevenses near Roundthwaite (elevenses are an important part of any 'End to End'). There were a few spots of rain on the road to Tebay Services, along which there were beautiful orchids flowering.

At Tebay we stopped and enjoyed a lovely frittata snack. The rain, so far, was short-lived, and much enjoyed by the multicoloured Tebay ducks. It looked like we'd make the last two miles before the heavy rain set in.

The remaining route consisted of two poorly marked bridleways. To get onto the first I had to undo two pieces of orange string holding a gate shut; the knots were fiendish, and I had to use my teeth. The second bridleway was longer and took me back onto the line of the Roman road. We were in sheep country – and the views of the hills were awesome!

At Thunder Stone Farm cattle grid we had our earliest finish so far. A thunder stone is the name given to a large erratic boulder in this part of Cumbria; you see them strewn across the landscape. No one knows for sure how they came to be there, whether brought by geological forces or erected by early inhabitants as markers of some sort.

The rain soon came down and lasted the rest of the day, but once again the Creator had been my Helper, my Guide and my Way.

From Psalm 121:

I look at the mountains;
where will my help come from?
My help will come from God the Maker,
who will not let me fall and is always awake.
However many generations have passed this way,
the mountains and hills have always been there.
Our songs may be short but their songs last forever.
The paths may be temporary but God keeps watch.

Action:

Why not try writing some kennings this Lent? Kennings are Anglo-Saxon word pairs. The kennings that follow were inspired by Psalm 121. They will give you the idea. The whole is a playful way of reflecting on scripture on any journey.

Horizon watcher,
Help seeker,
Hope assurer:
Cosmic Creator.

Doze denier,
Side guarder,
Planet revolver:
Wakeful Protector.

Day unfolder,
Night reposer,
Danger disperser:
Forever Keeper.

Janet Lees

Third Week of Lent, Monday

Bible reading:

From Mount Hor they set out by the way to the Red Sea, to go around the land of Edom; but the people became impatient on the way. The people spoke against God and against Moses, 'Why have you brought us up out of Egypt to die in the wilderness? For there is no food and no water, and we detest this miserable food.'

Numbers 21:4–5 (NRSV)

Reflection: The wandering, grumbling people of God

This story, of an alien people on a long-ago journey, came alive for me when the minister of the inner-city church I attended (Donald Eadie, in Notting Hill Methodist Church) preached on 'the wandering, grumbling people of God'.

Wandering can be romantic. Grumbling is down-to-earth. In Notting Hill – before it became posh – there were plenty of reasons for complaint: poor housing, racism, poverty, unemployment or job insecurity, pollution, violence on the streets. And my fellow worshippers were frank about these. But there was also much mutual support and times of celebration; like community meals, where everyone brought what they could: curries and coleslaw, soup and samosas, fried chicken and flapjack, Persian rice and American cornbread, delicious food made to family recipes from all over the globe. Memories and nourishment were shared generously. So we weren't actually in any position to say, 'We detest this miserable food'!

Life was often hard for those who, for one reason or another, were living in exile. Because we were part of a caring community, we were not lost in the wilderness. And yet, like the children of Israel – who asked, 'Why have you brought us up out of Egypt to die in the wilderness?' – we still did question God. We grumbled to each other and we grappled with God: about the social problems mentioned above and about personal issues like mental health, family breakdown, the looming problem of AIDS. That questioning

(I see now) was the way we did theology. So when Donald preached about 'the wandering, grumbling people of God', he was thinking of us too.

But this passage from Numbers raises many other problems for me. The lectionary passage (Numbers 21:4–9) starts just after the Israelites made a bargain with God to help them conquer the Canaanites and destroy their cities. This kind of history 'with God on our side' fills me with questions. And now another question: when the people protested, 'then the Lord sent poisonous serpents among the people, and they bit the people, so that many Israelites died'. So now I find myself questioning a God who doesn't like being questioned, and who responds with violence.

The story goes on: the people repented, Moses interceded and God told him to have a bronze snake made and displayed on a pole. People who looked at that would be healed of their snakebites. Can you hear me grumbling again? I really am in the wilderness. What is all this about? A strange totem, an inexplicable cure … thousands of years ago it might have made sense. But today?

Yet today we still see the image of a snake twined round a rod: on medical publications and buildings like hospitals. The Rod of Asclepius is an ancient Greek symbol of healing. In Greek mythology, Asclepius was the god of medicine and healing. That symbol is recognised today. But (I'm still wondering and wandering) what has that got to do with Moses? Maybe this is an archetype. In very different cultures and situations, symbols and meanings can connect. The bronze snake reminded a dislocated and distressed people of God's power to heal. That story would have been remembered generations later by someone like Nicodemus, hearing Jesus' words, 'And just as Moses lifted up the serpent in the wilderness, so must the Son of Man be lifted up' (John 3:14). 'Lifted up' is not about power, but about healing. For future generations of Christians, these words came to signify the love of God lifted up on the cross.

Today, in a few verses from an often baffling, sometimes alienating, Old Testament book, we've seen a people (like us today) struggling to survive, challenged in their faith, protesting to their leaders, sometimes rebelling. We've glimpsed the angry God in which they believed, who is also still there as a healing presence for this wandering, grumbling people on their long journey.

In the Book of Numbers (6:24–26) there's also an ancient blessing, attributed to Aaron and still used today. So let peace have the last word:

The Lord bless you and keep you;
the Lord make his face to shine upon you, and be gracious to you;
the Lord lift up his countenance upon you, and give you peace.

Jan Sutch Pickard

Third Week of Lent, Tuesday

Bible reading:

Happy is everyone who fears the Lord,
  who walks in his ways.
You shall eat the fruit of the labour of your hands;
  you shall be happy, and it shall go well with you.

Psalm 128:1–2 (NRSV)

Reflection:

'Happy' are we who used to be 'blessed'. In earlier English translations of the Bible we were usually 'blessed' but lately we have been mainly 'happy'. In the 17th-century 'Authorised Version', Psalm 128 opens by telling everyone who fears God that they are 'blessed' and closes with another promise of divine blessing.

Like other words rooted in an ancient sacred culture where the divine was everywhere and everyday, the word 'blessing' has left its religious moorings. It's used in many ways which seem disconnected from faith. 'Bless him' we say of someone or, 'Ah bless …' We still share explicitly religious blessings, but usually in an explicitly religious environment. When the Priest raises her hand to trace the outline of a cross at the close of a service, a blessing is invoked on everyone present. A blessing may be a potent moment when the bestower has a sense of what she is bestowing and the recipient understands they are covered in this intentional sign of love.

I noticed this dramatically a few years ago, walking with the Irish poet and philosopher John O'Donohue, when someone recognised him and made a spontaneous and unusual request: 'Will you bless me, John?' John gently raised his hand and recited some spellbinding mystical poem of grace upon him. His serious intent conjured up a kind of blessing forcefield in which we were all caught. Sometimes a blessing is like a holy spell.

Our English word 'bless' was shaped by the Latin root of benediction, meaning to speak well of, and a blessing is more than simply praising or extolling someone. It is about wishing them well from God, about wishing God on their life and in their life. In his final book, *Benedictus*, a miscellany of unexpected blessings, John took the notion of blessing out of the church and into the world. He wrote 'A blessing for a farmer' and one 'For a nurse'. Blessings for 'The parents of one who has committed a crime' and for 'One who is exhausted'. 'A blessing for one who holds power' and 'A blessing after a destructive encounter'. 'A blessing for old age' and one 'For an addict'.

In what Christians call the 'Old' Testament, people thought of being 'blessed' as being favoured by God and to bless someone else was to wish they too might know God's favour. In the creation story God blesses all creatures. Later God tells Abraham and Sarah to leave their land and travel to another. 'I will bless you,' says God, 'and people everywhere will be blessed through you.'

Blessing became a central motif in the Bible, what Walter Brueggemann calls *'a force of well-being active in the world'*.[1] People came to understand that the life force of creation makes abundance possible, that God's good earth is meant to be a blessing for all. We are not meant to be poor or downtrodden or hungry or lonely. We are not meant to be abandoned or thirsty or broke or ill. We share a good universe where there is enough for all. A blessing is about sharing the good life that God provides.

The song 'Blessed', by the American singer Lucinda Williams, is a litany of the unlikely blessed – ordinary, marginalised, unnoticed people – and how they bless us. The blind man, the teacher, the battered woman, the soldier. She sings of people bestowing blessings in the way they live their lives – becoming the means of God's kindness by the kind lives they live. They are a blessing because they are sharing around God's abundance. They are God wishing everyone well. They are not the celebrated or honoured, not the powerful but the overlooked. They may not be religious and often they are not. '... *A blessing does not confer holiness*,' says Barbara Brown Taylor.

'*The holiness is already there … Because God made these beings, they share in God's own holiness, whether or not they meet your minimum requirements for a blessing.*'[2]

In blessing each other we bless the invisible God. Being blessed by each other we know, ourselves, the blessing of God. Blessed is everyone who walks in God's way.

Martin Wroe

Notes:

1.   From 'The Liturgy of Abundance, the Myth of Scarcity', an essay by Walter Brueg-gemann: https://www.christiancentury.org/article/2012-01/liturgy-abundance-myth-scarcity

2.   From *An Altar in the World*, by Barbara Brown Taylor, Harper One, 2009, p.203

Third Week of Lent, Wednesday

Bible reading:

'Now in the law Moses commanded us to stone such women. Now what do you say?' They said this to test him, so that they might have some charge to bring against him. Jesus bent down and wrote with his finger on the ground. When they kept on questioning him, he straightened up and said to them, 'Let anyone among you who is without sin be the first to throw a stone at her.'

John 8:5–7 (NRSV)

Reflection: He left us bowing down

He went to the temple to pray.
They came to hear him, and he taught them.
They came to test him and brought a woman
to humiliate in front of him.
She was caught in the act, but where was the other one?
I thought the act required two,
or maybe I'm overreacting,
being hysterical, too emotional.

He was praying, so he tried to focus by bowing down
and writing on the ground.
They said she should be stoned to death,
but not the one who was caught in the act with her.

'Stone her, if you wish,
but only you who have never done anything wrong,
never lied or cheated,
held anger or lust in your heart.
Go ahead and throw your stones,'
and he bowed again, back to praying,
writing on the ground.
And they went away,

one by one,
leaving him with the woman caught in the act,
humiliated and pardoned.
Her life was spared, his life was not.
Her sin was theirs, ours was his death.

No one could lift a stone, and so they left,
and he went back to praying,
then to dying,
and left us bowing down.

Prayer:

Holy One, Teacher of this Lenten journey,
when I read this ancient story
my heart weighs heavy as I think
of all the women
caught in webs of condemnation,
loved and hated for who they are;
and then I see you bent down,
writing on the ground.

It changes everything.

Jesus, guide me through these Lenten days,
that I may look within
when I am eager to condemn.

Rebeka Maples

Third Week of Lent, Thursday

Bible reading:

The whole congregation of the Israelites complained … in the wilderness …
Then the Lord said to Moses, 'I am going to rain bread from heaven for you, and
each day the people shall go out and gather enough for that day … On the sixth
day, when they prepare what they bring in, it will be twice as much as they
gather on other days … In the evening you shall know that it was the Lord who
brought you out of the land of Egypt, and in the morning you shall see the glory
of the Lord, because he has heard your complaining against the Lord …'

Exodus 16:2–7 (NRSV)

Reflection:

Wilderness is not an easy journey. The pathway may lead to the Promised
Land, but it commonly takes us through spiritual landscapes more difficult
than the place we originally left. Despite its imperfections, our place of
departure may seem richer in our memories than the barrenness of the here
and now. It's precarious to be on-the-way-and-not-yet-arrived, even more
so when the journey is arduous. Wilderness exposes us; it frames our vul-
nerabilities. Life hangs in balance.

Pilgrimage embraces two contrasting elements of the spiritual life: the
celestial destination and everyday provisions. If pilgrims live in the clouds,
they do so with both feet on the ground. We may not live by bread alone,
but we certainly can't live without it.

Wilderness is a place of hunger, and the Israelites were hungry. Slavery and
oppression compelled them to leave Egypt. Yet, in some ways, life in Egypt
was better than the wilderness. They were insufficiently provisioned for
the journey, and they lacked enough to eat. Wilderness on an empty
stomach could not be sustained.

What are the terms and conditions of a spiritual journey? Did the Israelites have the right to complain? Can disciples make suggestions? Can we file a grievance while following God? Or, is there an as-it-should-be quality to the pilgrim life? Should situations be accepted as they are, context left unchanged? Is submissiveness the key to spiritual transformation?

Perhaps it's permitted to point things out to God, to provide notice that life is lacking. We may be more focused on detailing the circumstances than holding out hope for change; yet, it is in precisely such moments that we meet the God of Surprise, who acknowledges our plight and responds, who does what we ask and then some. 'Nourishment? I can provide it. Daily food? I can make that happen. I will rain bread from heaven, and you can gather what you need.'

God didn't just give – God gave with an eye on the prize. In providing the Israelites with desert sustenance, God linked resources to remembrance, blessings to memory: the manna was a reminder that the Lord had brought the people out of Egypt, that the God of provisions was also the God of redemption. Blessings remind us of the comprehensive reach of God, that past deeds, present grace and future promise all stem from the same benevolent being. To be in the wilderness is to glimpse the fullness of God.

Moreover, God determined that every day would not be the same. For five days, they would gather what they needed, but on the sixth day, they would double the amount, which would supply day seven as well. On the Sabbath, one shall neither work nor worry.

In the wilderness, we tend to focus on place. How do we get out of there? Where is the Promised Land? Yet, God marks the wilderness with sacred time. Five ordinary days, a day of preparation and the seventh-day finale. A day of rest is wise on a wilderness journey, but rest – and resting in order to continue the journey – is not the primary purpose of Sabbath. Rather, God rested on the Sabbath because the world was complete. The day evokes completion and fulfilment. It prefigures our ultimate arrival, when human needs are met through spiritual union with God and others. It is a day of abundance and perfection, a time-based projection of our destinational arrival. Sabbath provides a slice of the Promised Life.

God met the Israelites' request with more than temporary, physical provisions. He linked blessings to memory, and cyclical time to union with God. It may have taken the Israelites forty years to get out of the wilderness, but the manna reinforced the spiritual mystery that once a week the Israelites were exactly where they should have been, experiencing the Sabbath as a foretaste of life beyond the river.

Questions:

Lent is a time of keeping our eye on the prize, an exercise in remembering the benevolent acts of God. How do daily blessings and sacred time sustain you when you are on-the-way-and-not-yet-arrived? How does the daily act of gathering prepare you for a Sabbath glimpse of the Promised Land? What gifts of God will you gather today?

Rodney Aist

Third Week of Lent, Friday

Bible reading:

For the Lord is a great God,
  and a great King above all gods.
In his hand are the depths of the earth;
  the heights of the mountains are his also.
The sea is his, for he made it,
  and the dry land, which his hands have formed.

O come, let us worship and bow down,
  let us kneel before the Lord, our Maker!
For he is our God,
  and we are the people of his pasture,
  and the sheep of his hand.

Psalm 95:3–7 (NRSV)

Reflection:

When I read the Psalms, I often hear in my mind the words of the Psalter and their plainsong chant, learned more than fifty years ago. Now, as I read this version of Psalm 95, it is those traditional words that come to the surface instead. The Psalmist tells of an awesome God, to be worshipped for his marvellous creativity, his authority above all other gods. He is majestic, glorious in splendour, yet the compilers of the Psalter draw us to consider the works of his hands in ways that are domestic and intimate. God holds in his hands, they tell us, not the 'depths' but all the 'corners' of this earth and his hands have 'prepared' the dry land for us to inhabit. It is the language of the homemaker. The preparation of somewhere for us to live safely; the corners of life, held in mind. The corners: the forgotten places, the obscure, the dusty, the out-of-the-way.

Jesus himself came to an obscure corner of the Mediterranean, to a people who were not special, just loved. So, he reaches to the earth's corners: to the forgotten ones, the nameless ones, the ones that life has crushed into the dust. It is for them that his hands have prepared a safe landing, a rescue from the turbulence of life and the overwhelming waves of oppression or grief. If not in this life, then their consolation is certain in the next. Not one person will be overlooked. His hands bear the scars of that costly preparation. He will not cease to search out and salvage humanity from the overlooked corners of our earth, holding the nameless child pulled from the rubble of Idlib; the family driven from their home in the remote Amazon rainforest; the terrified girl forced into child marriage; the prisoner waiting on death row; the mother who cannot save her baby from famine or disease. He holds the corners of the earth and the heights of the mountains and the deep mysteries of the sea.

There are other kinds of corners too, the corners that trap us, where we find ourselves 'cornered', walled-in by the implacable prejudices and hatreds that create division and rend families, societies and nations apart. It is those walls, with their sharp and rigid angles, that are demolished by the cross, by the vulnerability of love, by hands that not only reach out to hold and form and protect, but willingly submit to anguish and to naileddown immobility in order to share and save our helpless human condition.

We are, in every sense, the sheep of his hand.

Love only

As the headlong race
Of time falters, will Love swallow
History and its intolerable sorrow?
Counterpoise mercy
Against the weight
Of all time's cruelty?
Or offer endless consolation
In fields of vast and ageless grace?

Pause upon life's threshold:
Stand here, beneath this great crossbeam,
Which bears the roof of stars and storm,
And wait for morning.

Janet Killeen

Third Week of Lent, Saturday

Bible reading:

Now when Jesus learned that the Pharisees had heard, 'Jesus is making and baptising more disciples than John' – although it was not Jesus himself but his disciples who baptised – he left Judea and started back to Galilee. But he had to go through Samaria. So he came to a Samaritan city called Sychar, near the plot of ground that Jacob had given to his son Joseph. Jacob's well was there, and Jesus, tired out by his journey, was sitting by the well. It was about noon.

John 4:1–6 (NRSV)

Reflection: Living on the edge; crossing boundaries

The fourth chapter of John's Gospel marks a significant turning point in his story. It relates a remarkable encounter between Jesus and a woman, by far the longest recorded in the gospels. He had been working with his disciples alongside John the Baptist's movement to call people to repentance, in the face of God's imminent judgement. It seems that Jesus made a deliberate decision to leave Judea behind, perhaps because at this early stage he didn't want to be drawn into a controversy about baptism, but more likely, because of a fundamental difference between John's message and his own.

To let go often involves difficult choices and a degree of courage. It carries the risk of being misunderstood, of causing hurt and offence. Jesus recognised his debt to the Baptist as one who prepared the ground for his movement, but saw the radical difference between John's severe message of judgement and his own teaching and practice centred on the God whose grace reaches out to all people and whose Kingdom is about healing broken bodies and minds, transforming lives, relationships and communities.

So he turns his face to the north. They could have taken the eastern route, crossing the Jordan River to avoid Samaria, a journey which would have taken twice as long as the more direct path through Samaritan country. The story intends us to believe that Jesus deliberately chose to cross that boundary. Just before the town of Sychar the road forks, one branch leading west towards Shechem (modern Nablus). Just at the fork stands Jacob's well. Genesis 33 tells the story of reconciliation between Jacob and his brother Esau, of Jacob's decision to cross the Jordan, settle in the area and buy land, which on his deathbed he bequeathed to Joseph (Gen 48:22). Many Jewish memories gather around this spot to which Jesus comes seeking refreshment. He crosses the boundary between Jewish and Samaritan land, scene of a conflict which had grown over 400 years, smouldering on, as bitterly as ever.

This racial hostility between Jews and Samaritans is reflected in the gospels, and even in negative attitudes expressed by the disciples themselves (Lk 9:54). Jesus challenged these attitudes. In the next chapter (Lk 10) he makes a Samaritan the hero of one of his best-known stories. In the encounter with the Samaritan woman Jesus converses with a woman who is not only a foreigner, but someone of dubious morality, thereby crossing several divisive boundaries at once. He was constantly breaking down walls of prejudice, fear and hatred; teaching and practising justice and reconciliation.

Although, tragically, hostilities continue today in different forms, there are projects in and around the city of Nablus which seek to bring people together across the divides, promising a better hope for the future. Project Hope seeks to engender a wider vision and in Balata refugee camp the Haneen (longing) Project seeks to empower women, providing training and marketing opportunities for the distinctive appliqué and patchwork designs produced in their homes.

As we reflect on these verses, and on contemporary society, we need to ask: What boundaries are we being called to cross? What risks is the Spirit prompting us to take, individually or with others, to help break down those dividing walls, and build bridges of reconciliation and hope? Just as Jesus did. All the time.

Prayer:

May we be willing to cross boundaries which divide,
and create conditions that make for
justice, peace and reconciliation.

Warren Bardsley

Third Sunday of Lent

Bible readings:

A Samaritan woman came to draw water, and Jesus said to her, 'Give me a drink.' (His disciples had gone to the city to buy food.) The Samaritan woman said to him, 'How is it that you, a Jew, ask a drink of me, a woman of Samaria?' (Jews do not share things in common with Samaritans.) Jesus answered her, 'If you knew the gift of God, and who it is that is saying to you, "Give me a drink," you would have asked him, and he would have given you living water.'

John 4:7–10 (NRSV)

… a spring of water gushing up to eternal life.

John 4:14b (NRSV)

Reflection:

It is a dramatic story. Jesus, on his way through Samaria, takes a rest in the town of Sychar. To begin with, he should have avoided passing through Samaria. It was not the correct ritual behaviour for a Jew. Speaking with a woman made it worse.

I remember my early participation in feminist theology groups. It was the time when we re-read many biblical texts from the perspective of women's lives and experiences. John 4 was a key text, embraced enthusiastically by many women: Jesus enters into a theological discourse with a woman, one with a shady reputation at that. In dialogue with this nameless woman Jesus develops his own theological position. Her questions are as important as his answers.

Of course we could also read John 4 from the perspective of mission theology: someone who knows, teaches another, who does not know. Lately theologians have offered new perspectives on the contribution of 'the other'. It is the witness of the woman that leads her community to overcome its cultural and religious bias against a Jew and to recognise that 'this is truly the Saviour of the world'. Personal witness to God's love and mercy, rather than teaching about God, became the new entry point to mission.

My own favourite entry point, however, is the story itself and the fact that it develops around the access to the fundamental necessities of life – food and water. Jesus, like everyone of us, needs to eat and drink. His disciples, the text tells us, had gone to town to buy food.

Jesus is resting by Jacob's well. He is firmly set in the tradition of his people, connected to the lasting presence of the fathers, drinking from the well of the common origins. And he receives the water from the hands of a Samaritan woman, 'unclean' hands.

But in the act of sharing what keeps us alive – water, food, a sense of identity, a word of encouragement in our common struggle for justice – hands and hearts are cleansed; we are renewed and strengthened to do good in this world.

Prayer:

God, wellspring of our lives,
we come to you thirsting for living water.
Make us strong to walk alongside those who lack access to clean water,
and those whose water has been stolen
and who are standing up for their rights;
open our hearts to share with those who have to struggle for food;
help us to welcome those driven away from their fields and wells.

God, meet us on the way, in the heat of the day;
let your justice roll down like a river of well-being for all;
let your peace well up in us like water from an everlasting source –
a spring of water gushing up to eternal life.
Amen

Action: See www.wateraid.org, www.christianaid.org.uk

Reinhild Traitler-Espiritu

Fourth Week of Lent, Monday

Bible reading:

The elder to the elect lady and her children, whom I love in the truth, and not only I but also all who know the truth, because of the truth that abides in us and will be with us forever.

2 John:1–2 (NRSV)

Reflection:

A recently published book was entitled *In Your Loving Is Your Knowing*. It was a tribute to, and a quote from, the late Elizabeth Templeton, Scottish theologian and teacher. Liz was a brilliant exponent of philosophy and logic, but the roots of her prophetic vision were grounded in the belief that truth was to be found in relationships, and above all religious truth could only be accessed by love. She was unsparing in her allegiance to this, and always saddened by those who saw acceptance of credal formulas as the entry points to the kingdom of God.

The link between love and truth was of course fundamental to the teaching and life of Jesus. What has been known as 'the Golden Rule' is based on love. In the gospel accounts, this always took precedence over the demands of religious observance that, in the hands of religious leaders, could often smother love. The history of leadership in the Christian Church has not been a good one. Centuries of division, and many lives lost, have resulted from judging and condemning the beliefs of other Christians. Liz Templeton challenged all this when she gave a talk to a gathering of the World Council of Churches in 1991, telling them that truth could not be fully measured in objectivity, but must be experienced in communion with each other and with God's world.

An unusual aspect of the second letter of John is that it is written to a prominent woman in the church. It assumes a place in the structure for women that has been dramatically absent in the nineteen hundred years since, and still is, in some churches. In fact the letter was only included in the Bible by some branches of the church centuries later. Many scholars consider this John to be the same person as the writer of the fourth gospel. If so, although all the other evangelists speak about Jesus' encounters with women, most of the disciples want to keep them away from him and them! The writer of this letter seems to be a rare example of a man in the church at that time who has a close, respectful and loving relationship with a woman outside his family.

'All You Need Is Love' was one of the most famous of the Beatles' songs. If we are fortunate enough to experience the variety of love as a child, a spouse, a partner or friend, a parent or grandparent, we know that love can never be measured or logically proved, because we simply experience it as true. That's what 'falling in love' is about. Sometimes we can't help it – even if we wanted to. We just know that it's true and authentic. This is why betrayal or abuse of that trust is far more wounding than damage done by strangers.

Douglas Templeton, Liz's husband, another academic and scholar, once wrote a book with the title *The New Testament as True Fiction*. The word 'fiction' may seem to be the opposite of truth. Yet in the book, Douglas compared the fourth gospel to a historical novel, which far from distorting the truth of the witness to Jesus, greatly enriched this. John was, more than any of the other evangelists, the supreme storyteller, echoing Jesus himself, a large amount of whose teaching was through stories. And what stories they were – opening a window to the most basic and universal truths. In every great religion stories occupy a central place and instead of seeing them as the opposite of truth (as has crept into our language – 'don't tell stories!') we should embrace them as the drama of relationships that they can be, and windows into a deeper truth than anything limited to provable facts.

Prayer:

God of truth,
you are the sun –
shining in the hidden places of our lives.
We are complicated people,
living in the half dark of our limited understanding.

We long to be understood,
but often do not recognise that need in others.
Seeking explanations for the perplexing events around us,
we sometimes fail to glimpse your truth –
in the compassion of a friend, in the generosity of a stranger,
in the innocence of a child, in the wisdom of maturity.
Your truth is illusive when we try to capture it –
in creeds or dogma, in rules and laws.
Yet we are overwhelmed by its simplicity
when life gives us a glimpse of it.
These moments are gifts:
sunlit, star-bright, young as a newborn baby,
old as the rocks in the Cairngorms –
as we explore the paths you beckon us onto;
recognising the integrity of others
as listeners, encouragers and peacemakers.

God of truth,
we would be your people –
interpreting your love among us,
recognising the authentic moments in a life where all are valued,
all are included, their truth affirmed, their uniqueness celebrated.
Following the path of Jesus into new ways of justice,
as we rejoice in the rainbow spectrum of humanity.
Amen

Iain & Isabel Whyte

Fourth Week of Lent, Tuesday

Bible reading:

*God promises to fill me
with honey from the rock.*

From Psalm 81 (my own remembered version)

Reflection:

During 2019 I walked from Land's End to John o'Groats in 117 days, including during Lent and Easter.

On Day 90 I walked to Kinlochleven via the Devil's Staircase on the West Highland Way. I wonder why there are so many 'satanic' landmarks in Britain: the Devil's Beeftub in the Southern Uplands, the Devil's Elbow in Derbyshire …

I started not far from Kingshouse, and the first section of the path to Altnafeadh, at the bottom of the staircase, didn't present any difficulties. It did offer some super views of Buachaille Etive Mor, the Great Herdsman of Glencoe, and from my remembered psalms I recalled 'the Holy One is my shepherd'.

My walk supporters, my husband Bob and daughter Hannah, were at Altnafeadh, clearly a busy spot on a summer Sunday morning, to fill my water bottles and make sure I had everything I needed for the big climb. The path began to curve steeply upwards and, higher up the climb, I could see my ant-like companions zigzagging backwards and forwards down below.

It's the sort of walk where you get to recognise each other, passing individuals and groups on the ascent as we rest and walk, walk and rest, all the way up. So rather than a Devil's Staircase, it had me in mind of Jacob's dream of a ladder stretching between earth and heaven, with angels going up and down. We made room for each other on the path and exchanged greetings.

It took me about an hour and a half to get to the top. The valley stretched out below me; the mountain flowers peeped out between the rocks: hare-bells, small orchids, sundew and heather.

The descent to the Kinlochleven side is longer than the ascent, and probably the longest descent of the whole 'End to End'. The path was better, possibly recently overhauled, and the fords across the streams easily negotiated. I was entertained by Caw and Grunt, the names I gave to two playful aerobatic ravens who were wheeling around in the blue sky.

Psalms are important to Benedictines like myself, as they are used as part of the regular cycle of worship. The phrase from Psalm 81 I remember best is the last one: 'with honey from the rock I will satisfy you'. It seemed to me that my rocky walk up the Devil's Staircase had been sweet and satisfying.

Prayer:

God of mountain and sky, maker of heaven and earth,
we dream of many things –
especially for justice and peace in the world
and the courage to play our part in it.
We are thankful for all those who have accompanied us in
the ups and downs,
on the steps,
the angels from many nations.
As we look up to where ravens fly freely,
lift our hearts for the next part of the journey.

My heart, my core, my centre:
animate me,
make me glad –
fill me with honey from the rock!

Action:

There's a lot of lovely honey about. Find some to taste. You only need a small amount. Where possible make it local or Fairtrade. Sit somewhere comfortable. Open the honey and spend a moment taking in the scent of it. Good honey smells of the work of the bees and the flowers from which the pollen was gathered. In silence, offer thanks for the flowers and the bees. Then dip your finger in the honey and taste it slowly. There are many synonyms of the word 'satisfy' (the word used in some Bible translations for the verse in Psalm 81). After you have tasted the honey: how does it make you feel? …

Janet Lees

Fourth Week of Lent, Wednesday

Bible reading:

… for my people have committed two evils:
  they have forsaken me,
the fountain of living water,
  and dug out cisterns for themselves,
cracked cisterns
  that can hold no water.

Jeremiah 2:13 (NRSV)

Reflection:

On one side is chaos: fast cars and aeroplanes, gas and oil, immediate grat-ification and consumerist temptation. On the other side is creativity: bicycles and sailboats, candles and paper, beautiful woodland walks and nights spent stargazing. Fall off on the side of chaos and life will be easy. We could get across the country in a matter of hours and across the world in a day or two. We could buy whatever we want, and it will show up tomorrow or perhaps even today. And yet … the forests burn, the ice melts, the weather becomes brittle and the earth's resources are ravaged. Choose to jump off on the side of creativity and life will be challenging but filled with wonder. It will take longer to get to work, but the scenery will be awe-some. Which side will you choose?

On one side is chaos: clingfilm and plastic bags, disposables and trash, sea-horses gripping cotton buds and turtles deformed by plastic rings. On the other side is creativity: homemade wrapping paper and tote bags, thermoses and steel straws, recycling and reusing in ever new ways. Fall off on the side of chaos and life will be convenient. We could pick up our shopping in a polybag and toss it in the bin when we're done with it. We could buy premade, shiny wrapping paper and fill our bins with it once the gifts inside have been revealed. And yet … the oceans become toxic, sea life dies in pain and sorrow and biodiversity is diminished. Choose to jump off on the side of creativity and life will be challenging but filled with wonder. It will take longer to wrap your gifts, but the process of making something yourself will be a priceless treasure. Which side will you choose?

On one side is chaos: nationalism and racism, homophobia and trans-sceptics, hatred of the other and stubborn idolatry of 'the way we've always done it'. On the other side is creativity: diversity and love, learning and growth, love of the other and opportunities for transformation. Fall off on the side of chaos and life will be predictable. We could enforce the hetero-patriarchy and ignore new perspectives. We could keep marriage between a man and a woman and send asylum seekers 'back to where they came from'. And yet ... the hatred grows, the intolerance hurts, and we are sending people to their deaths. Choose to jump off on the side of creativity and life will be challenging but filled with wonder. We will have to let go of our assumptions, but we will learn and grow and love and transform. Which side will you choose?

On the one side is chaos: cracked cisterns that can hold no water. On the other side is creativity: the fountain of living water. Our consumerism and normativity are cracked cisterns. It's not an intentional evil: we didn't intend to end up where we are, and yet ... like the Israelites before us we have turned away from God to rely on what we can do in our own power.

The fountain of living water simply exists: the world gives us all that we need. Oxygen to breathe, water to drink, fruits to eat. But we wanted more, so we asserted our power over the world, inventing cars, gas and oil, using resources faster and faster so that we could travel more, buy more, do more. Humanity is diverse and beautiful. People love deeply regardless of gender. People transition, modelling God's transformative possibilities. People migrate, graciously showing us more and more of God's image in humanity. But we wanted to be the best, so we asserted our power over people, marking out norms so that we could shun those who were 'different'. Slow down, turn back to the living water, enjoy the world and the people around you; do we really need more?

We are walking a tightrope. Look down. On one side you can see cracked, jagged, unforgiving cisterns. The land is barren and dry. On the other side you can see a beautiful living fountain and all sorts of people laughing with pure joy as they drink. Which side will you choose today?

Prayer/action:

Find 5 things in your home that you no longer use. As you examine them, ask for forgiveness for wasting God's resources. Spend some time working out how to reuse or recycle your 5 items. Feel the creative joy of God's grace.

Or: Write a list of 5 people, or identities, that you struggle to like or understand. As you write them down, ask for insight. Spend some time working out how you might learn more about those people or identities, how you might come to love them. Feel the creative joy of God's grace.

Alex Clare-Young

Fourth Week of Lent, Thursday

Bible reading:

... He leads me beside still waters;
  he restores my soul ...

Even though I walk through the darkest valley,
  I fear no evil;
for you are with me ...

Psalm 23:2–3,4 (NRSV)

Reflection:

The familiar words, known since childhood. Sung at school services, in different churches, heard in different languages, bringing comfort at funerals. Beautiful words of serenity and stillness. Words familiar, too, to Jesus.

A psalm of contrasting images: being led by still waters, as well as through dark valleys.

I think of two particular, and literal, dark valleys. One, many years ago, in the Cairngorms. A whiteout on the tops, problems descending to the valley floor – and suddenly realising that it was far later than we had intended. Darkness falling early. Steep steep sides of the valley with distant stars impossibly high above. The path obscured by snow and rocks covered in a sheen of ice. Torch battery failing. My companion falling, regularly, wanting to sit down and rest, stumbling unwillingly on, confused. The need to just keep going, to survive this. Hope at seeing lights ahead: surely a search party? We'd left a note of destination on the car. Despair at realising it was an illusion. So dark. Keep going, keep stumbling slowly on.

And another – a very different valley, this one. Walking alone abroad and hopelessly lost. The valley ahead should lead back to the village. It narrows; the sides close in; there is no way up to see where I am, to gain a wider view, no sense of perspective. Heat, a tangle of undergrowth and bushes, the smell of something dead rotting nearby, flies buzzing everywhere, hidden rocks. I feel panic rising, the urge to get out of here as fast as I can, tripping and flailing at thorny bushes. Going back only means being lost again. Talk to myself, try to be calm, check the map again. Just keep going. Random thoughts and fears, then a sudden happy, silly memory of a fridge magnet: 'The only way out is through.' Keep ploughing on. Trust that this will work.

As Jesus faced his own death, and walked the dark valley towards it, did he hold on to the words of the Psalm? Did he picture the still waters of Galilee?

In our own darkest valleys of fear, grief, despair and loss, how do we hold to the certainty of God's presence sustaining us?

How can we hold on to the knowledge that 'You are with me' amidst the anxious confusion of today? When fear is used as a weapon to maintain power by creating division and hate; when all that seems most beautiful and precious in our world is threatened; when the powers are more swayed by money and maintaining privilege than by the lives of those most affected by their decisions.

How can those in desperate situations hold on to that faith that they are not alone? Countless people in all the darkest places of the world. The woman struggling to maintain a family life in the midst of a city devastated by war. The family struggling to keep going through never-ending poverty and mental illness. The Palestinian going to harvest his olives and watching as the ancient silvery trees are ripped out of his land.

And in the dark valleys of fear: words to strengthen and sustain those speaking truth to power, those confronting all the forces of destruction, those working to challenge and heal bitter divisions. 'I fear no evil; for you are with me.'

Even there, knowing the odds are so stacked against you and your cause, recognising your smallness against those vast forces and overwhelming power. Something to cling to in the darkest times: the awareness of still waters, of quiet and peace, coexisting with the dark valleys.

In the darkness and desolation as we walk through this time of Lent, here is something to hold on to. Something to restore the soul, bringing refreshment and new life.

Meditation and prayer:

Think of the dark valleys you have walked through in life.
Hold before God those known to you facing dark times.
Remember the places of fear and hatred in our world.
Hold in the light those opposing and challenging
all that extinguishes hope.

And then close your eyes and picture still waters.
Fresh, clear, limpid, cleansing.
Reflecting light.
Revealing what lies beneath.

Jesus, walk with us through the dark valleys.
Guide us by still waters.
And restore our souls.

Christian MacLean

Fourth Week of Lent, Friday

Bible reading:

The Lord is my shepherd, I shall not want.
  He makes me lie down in green pastures;
he leads me beside still waters;
  he restores my soul.
He leads me in right paths
  for his name's sake.

Psalm 23:1–3 (NRSV)

Reflection:

When I spent a month on Iona back in 2001, it was lambing season. Each day, as I would walk around the island, I would stop and watch the lambs. Some were like babies, trying their first hesitant steps, not straying too far from the security of Mum's side. Others were more like toddlers with that first taste of freedom – running around, jumping over each other, playing games that almost looked like tag. The bigger ones were almost like teenagers, having to prove who was the fastest, the strongest, the bravest. I even saw groups that were playing 'king of the mountain', pushing and shoving for the high ground. They were a delight to watch!

But then I began to notice something interesting. In the midst of all their frenetic activity, in the middle of all their playfulness, if one of the mums said something, every lamb would stop and lift its head to try to figure out if that was *their* mum calling to them. And the ewes, as they walked slowly around the field, contentedly chewing on the grass, doing whatever it is ewes do, if they heard a lamb suddenly bleat, they would lift their heads to try to figure out if it was *their* lamb who was calling – in need, in hunger. Those walks and those encounters with those gentle creatures gave me a new perspective on the 23rd Psalm, which is beloved by so many of us.

Like those lambs, we are busy. We run around, playing our games. We are constantly leaping over others. We are determined to be the king of the hill.

Voices call to us, competing, conflicting voices. We pause, lift our heads, perk up our ears, and then either ignore the voices or listen to the wrong ones. And thus miss the one Voice that can make the difference.

For in the depths of our hunger for a genuine life, there is that One who calls, longing to take us to those places where we can be fed grace and hope. For in the craziness of our overwhelming lives, where we just don't seem to have a moment for ourselves, there is that One who calls to us, over and over, to show us those thin places where we can rest, be at peace, and hear God's heart beating with ours. When our souls are parched by the words spoken by others which have turned to ashes, there is that One who hands us a cup of cool, living water. As we walk through all those valleys filled with the shadows of despair, illness, loneliness, and even death, there is that One who takes us by the hand and refuses to let go, ever.

When we think that we are surrounded by those who could care less, there is that One who is busy laying out a picnic, inviting us to come and celebrate the feast of life, even with our enemies.

When we think our lives are half empty, and we are about to knock them over, we find our hearts overflowing with mercy we are not sure we merit, with love which transforms our bitterness into compassion, and with grace which we can offer freely to those around us.

And surely, surely as we draw closer to the end of our days, we discover that goodness and mercy are the faithful companions who have always been with us, as we wander down that winding road home.

Though I find myself
sinking in the sea
of stress and success,
   you buoy me
   with your living waters
   until I am at
   peace;

though I run down
endless corridors

late for never-ending meetings,
   you detour me
   onto the walkways
   leading to your
   joy;

though I stumble through
the thorn-bushes of a
culture which seeks
to tear my soul to shreds,
   you prepare a picnic
   in the garden of
   grace;

though I am famished
and malnurtured from
wandering the shadows
of sin and death,
   you hand me a slice
   of life's bread slathered
   with the sweet honey of
   hope;

though I try to flee
from the very life
I convince myself
I am seeking,
   you slow me down so
   goodness and mercy
   can catch up with me and

push me
   into your
      heart.

Thom M Shuman

Fourth Week of Lent, Saturday

Bible reading:

*Then Samuel said, 'Bring Agag king of the Amalekites here to me.' And Agag
came to him haltingly. Agag said, 'Surely this is the bitterness of death.' But
Samuel said,*

> *'As your sword has made women childless,*
>   *so your mother shall be childless among women.'*

And Samuel hewed Agag in pieces before the Lord in Gilgal.

Then Samuel went to Ramah; and Saul went up to his house in Gibeah of Saul.

1 Samuel 15:32–34 (NRSV)

Reflection:

What is this?

Choose one reading from the Revised Common Lectionary for Saturday 21
March, the brief said. I duly look up the texts for this, a rather nondescript
day somewhere in the middle of Lent. The first reading is Psalm 23. I am
delighted. I love Psalm 23; it is my favourite psalm. It has accompanied me
in times of deep sorrow and great joy and spoken to my heart equally in
both. It is truly a psalm for all seasons. I could reflect on why this should be.

Or here is a gospel passage for March 21, and not just any passage, but the
first nine verses of John's Gospel, the Prologue, always the Christmas
gospel. 'The light shines in the darkness, and the darkness did not overcome it.' This poem of such great beauty and simplicity, yet cosmic in its
reach, would always repay reflection.

But here, like a thorn between two roses, is this utterly hideous little passage
from First Samuel. What is it doing here? And why, instead of choosing to
reflect on texts which are both beautiful and personally meaningful, do I
feel an overwhelming obligation to tackle this very unpleasant one?

So be it. My knowledge of Samuel is broadly limited to the Sunday school retelling of the boy Samuel being called by God to be a spokesman for the Lord and knowing that Samuel is the last of the judges, and the first great prophet since Moses.

But the passage requires a much more detailed knowledge of context to make any sense. To cut a very long story short, the book is part of the continuing theological history of the Israelites, composed around 630–540 BC. It seeks to explain God's law for Israel under the guidance of the prophets, and recounts the call of Samuel, the oppression of Israel by the Philistines, and his subsequent anointing of Saul as Israel's first king. Saul proves an unworthy king, he is replaced by David, whose son Solomon builds the temple in Jerusalem, and brings the Ark of the Covenant there. God then promises David and his successors an everlasting dynasty.

This passage comes as part of a chapter explaining how Saul proved himself unworthy. Saul has been ordered by Samuel, speaking on behalf of the Lord, to punish the Amalekites, one of the local warring tribes, for opposing the Israelites when they came up out of Egypt. Saul is commanded to attack them, and destroy them utterly: 'kill both man and woman, child and infant, ox and sheep, camel and donkey'. This, according to Samuel, is the word of the Lord. And Saul does indeed undertake this slaughter. But his mistake was that he did not kill the Amalekite king, Agag, and he kept the best of the livestock – the text reads 'all that was valuable; all that was despised and worthless they utterly destroyed'. Samuel, however, is not happy. Saul has not carried out God's order in full, but has tried to profit himself from it. He is disobedient, he is no longer fit to be king. And in a prime example of those who live by the sword perishing by the sword, Samuel finishes the job, and hacks the luckless Agag to death.

To a modern ear, this whole story is quite nauseating, and makes a very good case for those who believe that religion is the greatest single cause of human cruelty and suffering. Did the lectionary compilers wish to lead their readers to the conclusion that Jesus is not this kind of God, but actually like the good shepherd, or the shining light? This does not compensate for all these 'worthless' murdered children. To me, this is just a story of barbarous warring tribes all trying to justify the things they do in their own interests. Samuel is not the last man to have said 'God told me to do it.'

It is a hard thing to admit the truth of this, to recognise the extent to which violence, injustice, oppression and cruelty are most powerful when their perpetrators are most convinced of their own righteousness, their own justification. And after all, children are still hacked to death today; this story is not confined to the distant past.

We who are habitually scandalised by everyone except ourselves, see this more clearly in others, less so in our own small justifications. Lent is a journey towards recognising our complicity – but also to seeing the way beyond it. This may include saying very firmly, 'This is not the word of the Lord.'

Prayer:

Preserve us from the defendedness that makes us vicious,
give us insight to see the structures of injustice by which we profit,
and grace to cherish all people in our vulnerability,
knowing that we all live within your love.

Kathy Galloway

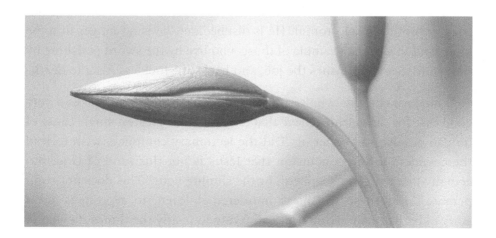

Fourth Sunday of Lent

Bible reading:

When they came, he looked on Eliab and thought, 'Surely the Lord's anointed is now before the Lord.' But the Lord said to Samuel, 'Do not look on his appearance or on the height of his stature, because I have rejected him; for the Lord does not see as mortals see; they look on the outward appearance, but the Lord looks on the heart.'

1 Samuel:16:6–7 (NRSV)

Reflection:

Samuel was sent to anoint the one God had chosen and would indicate to be the new king. He was sent to Bethlehem not to look but to listen for that guidance.

He would go on to anoint David, the shepherd boy, the youngest of Jesse's eight sons. David, a man after God's own heart who would one day dance with abandon before the Ark of God as it was brought into Jerusalem. David, a man with feet of clay who would also go on to commit adultery with Bathsheba and, unable to cover his tracks thereafter, would ensure her husband, Uriah, was killed in battle. David, a sinner, who would eventually bow before the Lord in confession offering the sacrifice of a broken spirit and contrite heart to the God he knew was steadfast in love and full of mercy.

David was whole-hearted to the delight of God and gained a kingdom.

The Lord does not see as mortals see. The Lord looks on the heart.

We can look in at ourselves, peeling back any facade to survey the landscape of our own hearts only to realise that we can never see as God sees; we can look below the surface but the truth is the full motivation and dimensions of our hearts escape our understanding.

When considering ourselves, like Samuel, we would do well to listen.

What will we hear?

Like Eliab, we might hear the clang and clatter of our own importance filling up the space, as we have forgotten our need for God. Yet as we remain still and allow the clamour to die down we may discern the gentle voice that calls us to 'Love the Lord your God with all your heart, and with all your soul, and with all your mind, and with all your strength' (Mark 12:30, NRSV).

We might catch the whisper of the Spirit prompting us to consider how we have or have not conformed to the will of God. Have we kept the outside of the cup and dish clean whilst allowing their inside to become dull and sullied by thoughts and desires that fall short of honouring the steadfast and merciful love we have received? Like David, do we need to bring the offering again of a contrite and confessing heart?

We might become aware of the sounds of uncertainty and insecurity that steal our joy and hold us back from responding to God's call to us to serve and rejoice in him with the same whole-heartedness that David did but, as we linger in that holy presence, we may also hear the beating wings of the dove at our shoulder as God declares to us that we are beloved.

The Lord does not see as mortals see. The Lord looks on the heart.

We can look out and ask what this means for how we consider others only to realise that we can never see as God sees; even if we try to look beyond the cover, we cannot judge, we cannot plumb the depths of any man or woman's heart to do so.

When considering the other, like Samuel, we would do well to listen.

What will we hear?

We might catch the strain of God's voice declaring his compassion for the orphan, the widow, the foreigner and the outcast.

Over the noise and distraction created by our differences, we might discern the voice of Jesus calling us to 'Love your neighbour as yourself' and to love one another as he has loved us.

We might hear the melody of Psalm 146 reminding us not to be dazzled or misled by glamour and celebrity; not to put our trust in princes, in mortal men, who cannot save, but to place our hope in the God of Jacob, the Maker of heaven and earth, who remains faithful for ever.

The Lord does not see as mortals see. The Lord looks on the heart.

Prayer:

Lord God, help us to be whole-hearted; may we be captivated by the beauty of your compassion and mercy; may we be transformed by the power of your steadfast love and grace; may we no longer be conformed to the pattern of this world but be obedient to your good, pleasing and perfect will. So, help us, Lord, as we look upon ourselves and the world around us, to listen for your voice calling us to show the same compassion and mercy, love and grace as we have received in obedience to your will.

Sarah Dickinson

Fifth Week of Lent, Monday

Bible reading:

justice (mishpat) is far from us,
and righteousness (tsedequah) does not reach us.
We hope for light, and behold darkness,
for brightness – but we walk in gloom …
Truth stumbles in the public square,
and uprightness (nakoah) cannot enter.

Isaiah 59:9,14b (NRSV, amended)

Reflection:

Chapters 56 to 66 of Isaiah date from between 538 BC, when Cyrus allowed the Jews to return to Palestine, and the rebuilding of the Temple in 521. This is a confused time. When the Temple was destroyed there were community laments. People ask God: 'Why do you not help?' Second Isaiah responds with a promise: 'Comfort, comfort my people!' (Is 40:1). There is the promise of a new and more glorious exodus. Cyrus is spoken of as God's agent (Is 45:1). But then many of the exiles choose not to return, and work on the Temple is slow to start. The laments continue. This chapter begins with a response to lament: God both hears and can save! (Is 59:1). But then the prophet turns to the people and argues that the reason for God's silence is the wickedness of society. Verse 9 takes up the lament and is followed by a confession of sin. This is the prelude to chapters 60 and 61, a new announcement of salvation, which Jesus takes up in the synagogue in Nazareth (Lk 4).

Many people feel that our own time is one of lament – lament at the damage done to creation which cannot be stopped overnight. In chapter 56 it is not the community but the leaders who are blamed. It is easy, and not entirely wrong, to look at Trump and Bolsonaro, at the leaders of the great corporations who let the planet burn so long, as it increases their profits. But as long ago as 1987 a prophet of our own day, Rudolf Bahro, warned that it was ultimately with family cars and washing machine detergents that we do the damage, rather than with bombs and nuclear power stations. A private house full of comforts, he said, underwrites the need for armaments, because the different standards between rich and poor nations make it a threatened luxury (*Avoiding Social & Ecological Disaster*). Lament turns back to the community and only makes sense if it leads to action – the theme of Isaiah 58. But what action are we talking about?

The writer of Isaiah 59 tells us that 'truth stumbles in the public square', and '*nakoah*', often translated as 'honesty', cannot appear. That rings many bells for us. We are surrounded by fake news and propaganda websites. Extinction Rebellion and YouthStrike say: 'Tell the truth.' This has provoked a furious backlash. People do not want their lifestyles challenged – the right to fly wherever they like, the right to do what they want. At the moment, in the first instance, the action needed refers to truth in the public square. In the midst of the fog in which we live there are places we can turn to. We can listen to Kevin Anderson of the Tyndall Centre in Manchester (you can find his blogs online), or to James Hansen, formerly the chief climate scientist for NASA (*Storms of My Grandchildren*, 2009). Or we can listen to Stephen Emmott, Professor of Computational Science at Cambridge, who was so worried by what he saw that he turned his graduate seminars into a play and put it on at the Royal Court (*Ten Billion*, 2012). These people are natural scientists who would like to be able to assure us that everything is just fine, there is no need to worry, and just carry on as normal. Unfortunately they can't. They look at the results of their research and say: humanity and the planet are in danger and matters are screamingly urgent.

Unlike 5th-century Jews we live in a 'democracy'. Of course it is threatened by oligarchy but the principle that we are responsible for the government we have still stands. Lament ('things are dreadful') leads to confession ('somehow we have allowed this to happen, and indeed we are part of it') and this leads to repentance ('we have to do something about it'). First seek out the truth, but then respond – in a new economy and a new politics which put creation and the future of all life on earth at the centre. The chapters which follow, Isaiah 60 and 61, tell us that 'in faith' this is possible, and is the concern of all those who believe in the NAME.

Prayer:

Holy Spirit,
Breath of Life,
help us to discern the truth and witness to it.
Fill us with joy and gratitude for your creation
so that we may honour it in all that we do,
serve it and keep it to your glory
and for our children
and our children's children.

Timothy Gorringe

Fifth week of Lent   89

Fifth Week of Lent, Tuesday

Bible reading:

I will praise the Lord as long as I live;
  I will sing praises to my God all my life long.

Do not put your trust in princes,
  in mortals, in whom there is no help.
When their breath departs, they return to the earth;
  on that very day their plans perish.

Psalm 146:2–4 (NRSV)

Reflection:

'Do not put your trust in princes' Okay. That's easy.

I already don't put my trust in modern-day 'princes' – be they politicians or global corporations or the 1% of the world's people who hoard half the world's wealth. I know there is little help there.

But for me, implicit in these verses is an admonition for patience: These people are going to die, so just wait until they do, then bad things will be sorted out.

I find patience is harder to come by as I grow older. Practically every Lent I try to make space for patience. That usually lasts for less than a week. I am simply not good at it. Because, for climate activists, patience is a pretty tall order. We can't wait for the 'breath to depart' and the 'plans to perish' of those mortals ignoring or actively contributing to the climate crisis. And though it is fine to remind us that when their breath departs, they will return to earth, chances are pretty good that on that day their plans will *not* perish. (Large corporations are good at succession planning, at not perishing, alas, even when the 'princes' do.)

We can't wait. There are people dying because of those 'princes', mostly people who contributed little to the problem in the first place.

So, what do we do?

The psalmist is clear: we first turn to God, praising God's steadfast love, alongside us as we wait for justice. But I wonder, do we need to dismiss all mortals as untrustworthy? Are there not others in whom we *can* put our trust? The youth of the world, increasingly active and informed and bravely telling truth to power; the research scientists, those who continue to monitor and warn us of the trending climate disasters and who work furiously to find creative solutions to mitigate the catastrophe; the non-violent activists, willingly arrested time after time, witnessing to inaction on the part of governments; our neighbours, who make the seemingly little changes – hanging out the laundry, eating less or no meat, turning down the thermostat – that nonetheless help; the community organisers who work for divestment from fossil fuels, subsidies for renewables, a price put on carbon; the few politicians willing to risk re-election rather than compromise their moral standards; indigenous people who, if we but ask, can teach us how to be a worshipping, contributing, affirming part of the non-human community surrounding us. There are people in whom there is help, people we can trust, preachers who preach, writers who write, artists who create – mortals helping us to acknowledge and face the crisis.

Again, we swing back to verse 2: 'I will sing praises to my God all my life long.' As I age, I find that life spins by faster and faster. Hence, my impatience. I want to make a difference. But as short as my life seems, as insignificant as a drop in the ocean, my praises join the chorus of other mortals – human and non-human – all of creation worshipping God. It is a chorus of joy, more reliable than the riches and powers of 'princes'.

Prayer:

Maker of the snow
swirling around the golden tamarack trees
outside my window,
teach me the patience of a snowflake
waiting to rest among its brothers and sisters on the ground

and of a tree waiting for spring's renewal.
Help me to seek out those whom I know I can trust,
that we may accompany each other in praise
and in the way of healing the planet and her inhabitants.
As Jesus walked alongside his friends,
help us walk alongside each other,
working for and praising God in his name.
Amen

Katharine M Preston

Fifth Week of Lent, Wednesday

Bible reading:

As Jesus went on from there, two blind men followed him, crying loudly, 'Have mercy on us, Son of David!' When he entered the house, the blind men came to him; and Jesus said to them, 'Do you believe that I am able to do this?' They said to him, 'Yes, Lord.' Then he touched their eyes and said, 'According to your faith let it be done to you.' And their eyes were opened ...

After they had gone away, a demoniac who was mute was brought to him. And when the demon had been cast out, the one who had been mute spoke ...

Matthew 9:27–30a, 32–33a (NRSV)

Reflection:

Two blind men, shouting their heads off for attention, following the preacher, demanding to be heard. You can hear them now – a clamour of insistence, which overrides even the excited racket of the crowd. And they broadcast the irresistible secret: you are the Son of David, the long-awaited, the King who brings deliverance. You are the Messiah who comes to release captives, give sight to the blind, who brings the uplifting of God to all who are oppressed. You have come to bring God's salvation to us, the prophets' promises fulfilled, the kindness of God, here and now, for us. 'Have mercy on us, Son of David!' Every eye will be fixed on Jesus now, because of the significance of that name and the age-old promises attached to that name. Promises and prophecies that have been learned from childhood and repeated in the synagogues. Everyone knows what it means. Excitement, expectation. The crowd buzzes, the religious leaders edge nearer to test for heresy: a press of people, some eager, longing, hoping, and yet others, hostile, cynical, defensive.

Somehow, Jesus manages to reach his destination and enter a house and the blind men follow him. What happens then is so familiar to us: the question that stirs faith, the touch that connects man and God, through which compassion and healing flows. Then, the moment of sight restored. What must that have been like for them? Or for those who watched and saw the slow dawn of seeing in sightless eyes? Their faces turned upwards towards a sky never seen before, and trees of leaf and shape and the whole wonder of life in all its fullness awaiting them outside. And crowding around them, men, women, children: faces whose expressions they must learn to read.

They tell us, these two shouting, determined men, that the vision of sightless eyes can sometimes see further than the sighted. Seeing 'with blinding sight'[1], they cannot hold back from shouting about what they see. How urgently we need their shouted words now, in our nation and in our broken world. 'Have mercy on us, Jesus, Son of David.'

There is a strange contrast in this passage too, because the next person who is healed is not shouting but locked in the prison of silence. Connecting, perhaps, with gesture, and maybe sounds that have no resemblance to speech. But cut off from that most precious of gifts, communication. Yet the inarticulate shouts of his innermost being are heard. In his silence, he too is healed.

You would expect compassion, joy, amazement to run like water among the crowd. That wonderful kinship of human beings when something amazing happens, those moments of oneness and shared, unselfish gladness. Three men miraculously healed, restored to life, to community. Tragically, the passage ends with the sour cynicism of religious leaders who see their status undermined, and maybe national stability threatened. We know the path their feet are on, and how it will lead to entrapment, betrayal, a garden invaded by armed guards, a show trial, and the slow torment of the cross. What they cannot see, but the blind men did see, and the dumb man knew without words, was that the Breath of God was already let loose in the world, blowing wherever he chooses, and no rock-hewn tomb and vast stone seal will be able to contain it. In shouting and also in silence, we hear it at work.

Riddle

I am road and traveller.

Darkest-before-dawn waiting
And the once-glimpsed star, flying
In shreds of cloud.
I am word and silence,
Shout and whisper,
Storm-sleeper, wave-walker.
I am tree and carpenter.
I turn the tables and rebuild the house.

I am rock and feather
And the falling sparrow.

I am the naked truth.

Janet Killeen

Note:

1.   Dylan Thomas, from 'Do not go gentle into that good night'

Fifth Week of Lent, Thursday

Bible reading:

Out of the depths I cry to you, O Lord.
   Lord, hear my voice!
Let your ears be attentive
   to the voice of my supplications!

If you, O Lord, should mark iniquities,
   Lord, who could stand?
But there is forgiveness with you,
   so that you may be revered.

I wait for the Lord, my soul waits,
   and in his word I hope;
my soul waits for the Lord
   more than those who watch for the morning …

Psalm 130:1–6 (NRSV)

Reflection:

This is one of the great penitential psalms always read in Lent, and should you like to read the six others, they are numbers 6, 32, 38, 51, 102 and 143. The central themes are the awareness of failure, the need for penitence and the assurance of forgiveness. Today when we mention 'sin' we can think of a hundred definitions! What is sin within our complex world order, let alone in our personal lives? Is my holiday flight a sin, given climate change? Is it right to take expensive cancer drugs when millions cannot get clean water? Is global capitalism in itself a sin, in that it also brings with it human suffering within poorer nations?

However we think of sin, Lent traditionally propels us to accept it as fact both in our own lives and in the life of the world. In these well-known penitential psalms we find the psalmist employing vivid imagery and language. In Psalm 32, he sings, 'While I kept silent (about my sin) by body wasted away; all day long my strength was dried up as by the heat of summer. Then I acknowledged my sin to you, and you, Lord, brought healing.'

I am conscious of my personal sin. I see its roots in a disconnection from the free gifts which I believe, through faith, God offers me; these include guidance, forgiving love, challenge, wisdom and a way of looking at the world which involves self-denial and spiritual discipline. Although I use the word 'disconnection' you will have your own understanding and language, but for us all the weeks in Lent give us an opportunity to review our spiritual life in various ways. This can be through silent meditation, or group Bible study or a guided retreat, or by renewed acts of compassion. At its heart, Lent is a time for followers of Christ to pause and to listen to the Spirit. To free themselves of the demands of the ego.

During one season of Lent, when I was leading worship, I wrote these words, suggesting that people use them at the start of each new day:

Lord, during this day in Lent
may I live in the knowledge that the universe is holy;
that all people are one in you;
that creation reflects your goodness,
and that when I seek your light and truth
my soul is at peace.

There is an old saying: 'For God to hear his people is to help them.' It is a comforting thought, and true. Perhaps that is why this wonderful imagery of the watchmen waiting for the dawn is so appropriate. Here were folk in the dark of early morning scanning the horizon in anticipation. Waiting for the single line of light, far in the distance, to suddenly illumine the darkness. They knew it would come, the beauty of dawn, and they also knew that with their Lord, however much they felt in the depths, forgiveness and healing was at hand. May we be reminded of an ancient prayer:

Almighty God,
give us grace to cast away the works of darkness
and to put on the armour of light,
now in the time of this mortal life.

Peter Millar

Fifth Week of Lent, Friday

Bible reading:

Then the seventh angel blew his trumpet, and there were loud voices in heaven, saying,

'The kingdom of the world has become the kingdom of our Lord and of his Messiah, and he will reign forever and ever.'

Revelation 11:15 (NRSV)

Reflection:

As a lifelong student of history, I am well-acquainted with kings, queens and family dynasties which ruled for centuries. I know the development of the notion of the divine right of the king/queen. I know from readings and courses that there were good and generous royals who really did want to do what was best for their people and kingdoms. And there were those who were, well, the very worst thing possible that could have happened.

And because these people have been relegated to the dusty pages of history, we feel they have no real connection with us. It is the same when scripture mentions 'kingdoms'. Because we live in places where leaders are elected by the people (us!), such things have no relevance to our lives, we believe. So when the Book of Revelation comes along and basically says that we have a choice as to which kingdom we want to be a part of, we just brush past and keep on reading, or close the book and do something else.

Yet, although we may not live in kingdoms, we still face that ancient choice.

In just the last few years, in more countries than one might imagine, people who were elected to provide leadership to their nation have suddenly begun acting more and more autocratic. They have begun to claim that they have an 'absolute right' to do whatever they want. They claim that they are not accountable to anyone.

Yes, over the decades more and more kingdoms have disappeared from our world. Oh, there is still royalty, mostly figureheads or objects of obsession of a public who can't get enough of them. But now, we have autocratic leaders who seem to be trying to set up new kingdoms – where loyalty to them, blind loyalty, is the most important quality of those around them. And so, like our counterparts in Revelation, we need to decide what sort of kingdom, what sort of a community, we will support.

The easiest choice is to simply offer that demanded blind loyalty; to simply accept whatever leaders say, whatever they tell us, whatever they want to do. To simply give in to despair and resign ourselves to being unable to do anything about the situation.

But we are called to make the harder choices.

So, when others want to build kingdoms of cruelty and indifference, let us make the harder choice to be a part of a community of compassion – to be those people where the needs and the lives and the hearts of others come first.

When the fearmongers offer hate as the power to control our lives, let us make the harder choice to be a part of a community of weakness – to be willing to serve others rather than have them serve us, to see the God-given value and gifts in each person.

When the autocrats see nothing wrong in ignoring the most vulnerable, in turning their backs on refugees and asylum seekers, while they side with the other bullies of the world, may we make the harder choice to live in communities of justice. To stand up to oppressors, to be willing to challenge the structures of power, and to make sure that the voices of those who are never heard echo through the corridors of power.

We face the same choice that our sisters and brothers faced 2000 years ago.

Let's offer community as an alternative to the kingdom-builders of our time.

Prayer:

You could have handed out
volumes of complicated theology,
but you call us:

to find community in those we overlook,
to welcome hope offered by the broken,
to be rich soil for the seeds of the humble,
to see justice as the feast of heaven,
to make compassion our language of love,
to see God in the faces of the most vulnerable,
to welcome everyone, and hurt no one,
to learn reconciliation from those we have tossed aside.

Thom M Shuman

Fifth Week of Lent, Saturday

Bible reading:

Then he led them out as far as Bethany, and, lifting up his hands, he blessed them. While he was blessing them, he withdrew from them and was carried up into heaven. And they worshipped him, and returned to Jerusalem with great joy; and they were continually in the temple blessing God.

Luke 24:50–53 (NRSV)

Reflection:

We needed some kind of ending. Even though we knew this was no kind of ending at all. We were coming to understand that if his arrival, according to those who still talked about it, didn't mean that he hadn't already been with us, neither need his departure mean he would now be leaving us.

I can't remember that much about the last time I saw him. He lifted up his hands and blessed us. That's the bit I remember. When you receive the blessing, the details can get a bit blurred.

I wasn't particularly thinking that he had left us. He was often vanishing into the moment. Ever since we'd known him he'd had a habit of disappearing for a few days, and then reappearing, often with someone you'd never met. He brought people together, unlikely people. He liked company as much as he liked getting away; he liked noise, he liked quiet. He didn't keep the usual boundaries. They sort of collapsed into him. He wasn't a personality type; you never had his number. He was always surprising you. Confounding you. Breaking down barriers. Between women and men. Faith and doubt. Holy and unholy. Tears and laughter. Death and life.

There was a moment when we thought he might be about to disappear for good. A long weekend. A Friday, a Saturday. So when he turned up on that Sunday it felt like he'd broken down the biggest barrier of all. That he'd collapsed the final wall in human existence, the one between presence and absence.

He'd always been present but now he seemed more present than ever. After that, we were rarely surprised to find him with us. And rarely alone when he wasn't. It was as if he left his presence with us to accompany his absence. We were getting used to the idea that perhaps there might be less of a distinction between the two. Maybe life was more of a continuum, less either-or and more both-and.

So on this misty day on the hill, we're all looking up. (Full disclosure: all we had to work with was this B-movie, triple-decker universe idea with heaven up there, the other place down there and all of us here in between.) And my guess is that when we were all looking upwards, he went sideways.

Disappeared into the moment again.

Into a refugee camp. Into a trench in a world war. Into a prison cell in which a writer has been disappeared. Into an overloaded raft trying to cross a sea between continents. Into a makeshift hospital where the medicine has run out. Into the eyes of forgotten and desperate people in the centuries to come, and the ones already past.

Always slipping away unnoticed.

At the time you could think of his leaving in terms of up and down, climbing from this visible world into some other less visible one. But these days we think differently, how he had to leave somewhere in order to be present everywhere. Now I don't think of him leaving earth for space. It's not like he was leaving the physical for the spiritual, leaving time for eternity. Now I think of him as moving from being somewhere in particular to being everywhere in particular. Ascending into the ordinary heaven of every blade of grass, every hair on a head, every pebble on the beach, every prayer we try and speak.

One minute he was with us and the next he was with everyone. With everything.

He lifted up his hands and blessed us. That's the bit I remember. And he still does. Still becomes present when we least expect him. Is still everywhere in general but always somewhere in particular.

We needed some kind of ending. But that was us. I think he was trying to tell us that there are no endings any more.

Martin Wroe

Fifth Sunday of Lent

Bible reading:

… He called out in a loud voice, 'Lazarus, come out!' He came out, his hands and feet wrapped in grave cloths, and with a cloth round his face. 'Untie him,' Jesus told them, 'and let him go.'

John 11:43–44 (Good News Bible)

Reflection:

I still don't know what to make of what happened that day.
I'd been friends with Mary and Martha and Lazarus for years.
I'd met Jesus at their house many times.
He seemed relaxed there, able to chat and tell stories,
able to rest.

I knew that Lazarus hadn't been well recently –
but it still came as a shock to hear that he'd died.
I went over to their house in Bethany as soon as I was able,
to be with Mary and Martha.
Lazarus was a good man. He was a loving brother.
The three of them had shared a house for years.
I thought that they would miss him terribly.

After the funeral I heard Mary and Martha talking about Jesus.
They had sent him a message to tell him that Lazarus was ill,
but they'd heard nothing from him.
We all knew that Jesus was a healer.
If he'd received their message
why hadn't he come to Bethany and healed Lazarus;
why hadn't he come when they needed him most?

Four days after Lazarus had been buried we got word
that Jesus was on his way to Bethany with his disciples.
When Martha heard that Jesus was coming
she ran down the road to meet him.

I don't know what they said to each other
but she soon came back to fetch Mary.
All of us who were in the house with Mary followed them.

Jesus could see how sad Mary and Martha were
and he must have seen that many of us were in tears.
Soon Jesus was crying too.

Many people were wondering why Jesus had not come sooner.
Some asked, if he could make blind people see,
why couldn't he have healed Lazarus?
Others recognised in his tears
how deeply he had treasured Lazarus as his friend.

And then Jesus asked to be taken to the grave where Lazarus was buried.
And he asked for the stone at the tomb's entrance to be rolled away.
Martha, ever the practical one,
protested that the body had been four days in the tomb
and by now would be smelling,
but Jesus said something to her,
and then some of us rolled the stone away.

Jesus looked up, through his tears,
he seemed to be praying,
and then he said in a loud voice,
so that we could all hear:
'Lazarus, come out.'

I was stunned –
how could he ask that?
Lazarus was dead,
he'd been dead for days –
how could he come out?

But out from the cave stumbled a figure
wrapped in graveclothes,
with cloth round his face,
and Jesus said simply,
'Untie him and let him go.'

As I said at the beginning of my story,
I still don't know what to make of what happened that day.
It was beyond understanding.
Beyond anything I'd ever known or have known since.

I sometimes wish I could have been with Lazarus, Mary and Martha
and Jesus that night.
I wonder what they talked about after the rest of us went home.
I wonder if Jesus told them why he did what he did.
I wonder how Lazarus is coping with the way people look at him
and talk about him in whispers.
I wonder if the Pharisees and chief priests have heard what happened.
I wonder what Jesus will do next.
I wonder if I will meet Jesus at the home of Lazarus, Mary and Martha
again ...

Prayer:

I wonder, Jesus,
I often wonder at the stories in the gospels.
I wonder what they tell me about what you are like.

I'm glad you had good friends.
I'm glad you had places where you could relax and feel at home.
I'm glad that your friends loved you and that you loved them.

May my home be a place of hospitality,
may friends feel welcome,
may strangers become friends.

Thought and action:

Is there anything you can do to make your home a more hospitable place?

This week, contact one of your friends who you haven't seen for a while.

Ruth Burgess

Sixth Week of Lent, Monday

Bible reading:

Let me hear of your steadfast love in the morning,
* for in you I put my trust.*
Teach me the way I should go,
* for to you I lift up my soul …*

Teach me to do your will,
* for you are my God.*
Let your good spirit lead me
* on a level path.*

Psalm 143:8,10 (NRSV)

Reflection:

How do we know God's will for us? What way should we live? The prophet
Micah, in 8 BC, wished to keep people alive to God's message and the realities
of love, compassion, justice and faithfulness to God. He wrote (Mic 6:8):

He has told you, O mortal, what is good;
* and what does the Lord require of you*
but to do justice, and to love kindness,
* and to walk humbly with your God?* (NRSV)

Jesus' teachings also guide us towards a better way of living, towards loving
our neighbour and incorporating loving-kindness into our daily lives. One
of the most famous of all Jesus' stories is that of the Good Samaritan (Lk
10:30–37). Jesus makes it very clear that it was the Samaritan's compassion
for and care of the wounded man that were so important, in contrast to
the narrow beliefs of the religious figures who had passed by 'on the other
side'. Jesus repeatedly broke the religious strictures of his day: he healed
on the Sabbath, touched the unclean and ate with tax collectors. He led a
life full of the practice of love for others. He taught that everyone is our
neighbour.

Archbishop Desmond Tutu in his writings describes the African word *ubuntu*, a word that is difficult to translate into English. *Ubuntu* describes a person who is welcoming, hospitable, warm and generous and willing to share. Could a word better describe the Good Samaritan?

Mahatma Gandhi, a Hindu, felt that one of the most important influences on his life was reading Leo Tolstoy's *The Kingdom of God Is Within You*. If that Kingdom is within us, then it may be that we can only enter the Kingdom when we live a life of love, kindness, compassion and gentleness. Gandhi and his supporters used non-violent resistance to overturn Colonial Rule in India. Years later in the USA, Martin Luther King Jr, inspired by Gandhi, also led a movement following the path of non-violence and civil disobedience in the fight for civil rights and to end racial inequality and segregation.

Owe no one anything, except to love one another; for the one who loves another has fulfilled the law. The commandments, 'You shall not commit adultery; You shall not murder; You shall not steal; You shall not covet'; and any other commandment, are summed up in this word, 'Love your neighbour as yourself'. Love does no wrong to a neighbour; therefore, love is the fulfilling of the law (Rom 13:8–10, NRSV).

Can we inculcate loving-kindness into our way of life; can we act justly and walk humbly with our God?

The last two verses of Kathy Galloway's hymn 'Life of the world' (CH4 141) read:

Oh, the life of the world is a source of our healing.
It rises in laughter and wells up in song;
it springs from the care of the poor and the broken
and refreshes where justice is strong.

So give thanks for the life and give love to the Maker,
and rejoice in the gift of the bright risen Son,
and walk in the peace and the power of the Spirit
till the days of our living are done.

Prayer:

Lord, like the Psalmist, help me to be aware of your steadfast love.
Help me in my search to know your will.
If it be your will, use me to be your eyes, your ears, your mouth,
your hands, your feet and your heart.
Let your loving spirit surround, infuse and lead me
this Lent and for evermore.
Amen

Allan Gordon

Sixth Week of Lent, Tuesday

Bible reading:

Save me, O Lord, from my enemies;
  I have fled to you for refuge.
Teach me to do your will,
  for you are my God.
Let your good Spirit lead me
  on a level path.

For your name's sake, Lord, preserve my life.
  In your righteousness bring me out of trouble.

Psalm 143:9–11 (NRSV)

Reflection: You heard me out

O my God, why did you hear me when I prayed?
You heard me and answered, without judging.
No one has ever done that for me before.

The vultures soared, eyeing their prey, a decaying corpse,
a lost soul roaming in the dark.
I think back to how I survived
and I wonder: why did you rescue me?
I lift my hands to heaven's door
for my soul thirsts when I remember that wasteland.

Come quickly, Spirit of my spirit;
do not hide from me or I will fall into that pit again.
Let me hear your song floating in the morning air,
filling my soul with your love.
Teach me the way when I am lost,
for I put all my trust in you.
You are my refuge; I hide under your wings;
teach me the way to walk with you.

O my God, you heard me when I prayed.
You saved me from all my troubles,
forgave me for my unforgiving deeds.
The predators who stalked my soul and devoured my body
were destroyed in your love.

Now I am your servant, not prey in the lion's den,
not caught in my enemy's trap.
O my God, you heard me out.

Prayer:

Forgiving God,
your love floods into my heart
and I know that my life has meaning,
but when clouds overshadow me with regret
and guilt pulls my soul down into despair,
I yearn again for your presence.
Remind me in these shadowy days of Lent
that you are near,
you walked this road
and know the way that leads to light.
Come, lead me now;
hear my prayer for resurrection.

Rebeka Maples

Sixth Week of Lent, Wednesday

Bible reading:

*At that time the army of the king of Babylon was besieging Jerusalem, and ...
the word of the Lord came to [Jeremiah]: Hanamel son of your uncle Shallum
is going to come to you and say, 'Buy my field that is at Anathoth' ... And I
bought the field at Anathoth from my cousin Hanamel.*

Jeremiah 32:2, 6–7, 9 (NRSV)

Reflection:

I write from Sarajevo, where I am spending a couple of months on sabbat-
ical. The sun is shining. I hear the sound of passing trams. Commercial
activity fills the streets. It's a temporary sojourn, and I feel warm and safe in
my short-term apartment. With a heavily layered history, East meets West
in Sarajevo. Along the city's pedestrian street, one steps from the Ottoman
to the Austro-Hungarian Empire. The Latin Bridge marks the site of Franz
Ferdinand's assassination and the start of World War One. Signs, symbols
and former venues recall the 1984 Winter Olympics, which brought the
world together at the height of the Cold War. In the aftermath of its com-
munist past, Sarajevo is a city of four religions. Diversity fills the streets.

While these layers remain influential, Sarajevo's primary memory is the
four-year siege of the city during the Bosnian War (1992–96). The city contains innumerable reminders – the odd ruin, pockmarks on buildings,
museums and photo exhibitions, memorial plaques and daily interpretative
tours. Without prompting, my host mentions the conflict. Scars remain,
both visible and invisible, and themes emerge: hunger and illness, fear and
horror, death and destruction. Thousands of adults and hundreds of children lost their lives.

To be under siege is to be surrounded by an enemy. To be cut off from provisions, severed from life itself. Siege is a violation of place, turning home
into a living hell. Siege calls into question life's most important values: hope

in the future, the sanctity of the present moment, continuity with the past. Siege desecrates the dignity of life and asks questions that often lack retort. Where is God? What's the future?

Jerusalem, too, was under siege. As King Nebuchadnezzar surrounded the city, Jeremiah prophesied that the city would fall into the hands of the Babylonians. There was no foreseeable future in Jerusalem. Survival lay in making a home among the enemy, living among the Other in Babylon.

Revelation is often incremental. We hear what we hear when we hear it, and God was still whispering in Jeremiah's ear: 'Your cousin is going to offer you a field. When he does, buy it.' Although the ground was shifting under the Israelites' feet and homeland was now a liability, Jeremiah followed God's counterintuitive advice: he bought a field on the outskirts of Jerusalem. When the future appeared to be a thing of the past, Jeremiah responded by holding his ground, a hope rooted in the promise of God: 'I will bring them back to this place, and I will settle them in safety. They shall be my people, and I will be their God.' Jeremiah's field was a time-based investment. Not now, but one day. Things will change, and transformation will occur. God's people will return to be planted in the land, and Jeremiah's meantime response was to hold his ground.

We don't have to be residents of Jerusalem or Sarajevo to feel under siege: by circumstances, by others, by our own self-doubts. The landscape is shifting, and we feel hemmed in, severed from life. Lent gives temporal structure to feeling under siege. Lent is a time of waiting, knowing that we are only saved through the grace of God. Lent is less about moving forward than it is about holding ground. Faithful perseverance. Staying where we are until the siege is lifted. Grounding our hope in what is yet to come: the dawn of Resurrection.

When Jeremiah bought the field, he was not chasing rainbows: he was weathering the storm until the sun shone again on the streets of Jerusalem, Sarajevo and the everyday places of home. Lenten faith is living in the meantime until God's people are safely settled.

Meditation and prayer:

Reflect upon the state of siege, the audacity of hope and God's call to hold our ground. How do we experience siege – as physical reality and spiritual metaphor – as part of our earthly journey, and how can we ameliorate the conditions of others? Imagine the lifting of siege as a resurrection image. Pray for the victims and penetrators of siege in places around the world, past and present.

Rodney Aist

Sixth Week of Lent, Thursday

Bible reading:

I thank my God every time I remember you, constantly praying with joy in every one of my prayers for all of you, because of your sharing in the gospel from the first day until now ... And this is my prayer, that your love may overflow more and more with knowledge and full insight to help you to determine what is best, so that in the day of Christ you may be pure and blameless, having produced the harvest of righteousness that comes through Jesus Christ for the glory and praise of God.

Philippians 1:3–5, 9–11 (NRSV)

Reflection:

How vital it must have been for Paul to know that his group of followers from Philippi was blossoming out there – beyond the walls of his prison – giving him strength to carry on. He could not see them, could not touch them, but he knew they were there and that they believed in him. In these initial salutatory verses, he expresses a particular fondness for the Philippians.

As I read these verses, my thoughts turn immediately to our Iona Community Family Group. Due to distances, we meet only once a year, for a full weekend together in the fall, with another, briefer check-in in June during our regional recommitment time. But, along with the daily group listed in the *Iona Community Prayer Book*, I light upon, one by one in my mind's eye, each member of our Family Group. 'Walk with them today, O God, and keep us on your way.' And I thank God every time I remember them.

Sometimes that is all we have as associates and members of the Iona Community: thoughts of one another witnessing, protesting, marching, working for peace, social justice and the integrity of creation in our respective churches, volunteer organisations and workplaces. The work of the Iona Community is so dispersed that at times, for some of us, it feels a bit lonely. Chances are, here in the States, that members of our churches have never heard of the Iona Community – except through us. They do not understand why we should have such an abiding feeling of warmth for and commitment to an unfamiliar movement founded during the Depression by a rather overbearing minister in Scotland, seeking the rather illogical challenge of rebuilding a ruined monastery from the early 13th century.

How can a 'dispersed' community work?

Just as a human family can feel the genetic, blood and experiential bonds binding them together across great distances, so too can members of an intentional group that seeks to love justice, love kindness and walk humbly with God feel bound together. That there is a shared organisation of prayers for our ministries, for parts of the world, and for each other, each day, strengthens those bonds. But strengthening us still is the thought that each of these people shares a commitment to peace, justice and the integrity of creation and is willing to vow to that. I don't know what each person is working at in his or her town, and I assume that the depth of the commitment varies with each individual. But I am bound to them through love, just as Paul was to the people of Philippi.

I am not sure what the 'day of Christ' is, and I suspect that I would not share Paul's anticipation that it was yet to come – as opposed to already here – but nevertheless, I pray for my Family members, 'that your love may overflow more and more with knowledge and full insight to help you to determine what is best'.

Prayer:

Dear God,
help us to plough and seed and weed the furrows we plant
toward a 'harvest of righteousness'.
Help us to remember that
in the shared labour of our communities
toward this common goal
we are strengthened and made whole.
Amen

Katharine M Preston

Sixth Week of Lent, Friday

Bible reading:

Be gracious to me, O Lord, for I am in distress;
my eye wastes away from grief,
my soul and body also.
For my life is spent with sorrow,
and my years with sighing;
my strength fails because of my misery,
and my bones waste away …

Be strong, and let your heart take courage,
all you who wait for the Lord.

Psalm 31:9–10, 24 (NRSV)

Reflection:

When he was 17, our son, Teddy, was living in a residential facility for people with mental and developmental disabilities. I was planning on taking him out one Saturday morning, and when I called earlier in the week to arrange that, the staff informed me that he had a lump on the side of his neck. So, I arranged to take him to see our family physician on Saturday morning. The doctor, who was also a friend, examined Teddy and said he thought it was an enlarged gland and would refer us to a specialist. About 12:30 that night, the doctor called me to say that he could not get to sleep – and wanted me to take Teddy down to the Children's hospital for immediate examination the next morning. We did, and long story short, they kept him overnight; and the next morning, after further testing by several doctors, we were told that Teddy had Stage 4 germ cell cancer. And thus, we began a journey that no child and no parents should ever have to take.

Teddy endured two major surgeries and six months of intensive chemotherapy before the doctors felt that they had got all the cancer.

I remember sitting in the waiting room while he went through his first surgery. It had been a whirlwind 24 hours from discovering what we thought was a minor issue was actually a life-threatening one; from talking with one doctor after another, until we sat around a table with all of them to hear that devastating diagnosis. And as I sat in that uncomfortable chair, flipping through magazines whose words and pictures I never noticed, I wondered 'How will we get through this?' And hope walked into the room in the guise of a friend, who simply came over and sat down next to us. And was with us until the operation was over.

I remember standing by the bed as Teddy was about to begin his first round of chemotherapy. What would it do to him? How would his body handle it? How could someone with limited cognitive abilities understand what was going on? Would hope be in that room, in that treatment? And then one of the oncologists came in, a young man who wore a yarmulke, and we just stood there in silence on either side of Teddy's bed. And then he simply reminded me that our common faith tradition called us to wait, in hope, for God. And then he left the room, leaving the gift of his hope in my heart.

I remember those sleepless nights spent in Teddy's room with him, watching the chemotherapy slowly drip into his body, listening to his soft breathing, hearing his occasional question, 'Am I going to die?' And I wondered if hope had simply abandoned him, and us. And then, a nurse would come in to check on him, take his vitals, and hold his hand, reassuring him that he was not alone, that he was surrounded by caring, compassionate hope.

I remember sitting in the family room on the oncology unit, taking a break from the fears, the worries, the hopelessness that threatened to seep into my heart and stay there. And a family would come in with sandwiches, snacks, or a home-cooked meal. Families who had been in this same place, in the same situation. They would share their stories, some of celebration and others of heartbreak. But as they left the room, I discovered that what they had really fed me was hope.

Long ago, this unnamed psalmist, going through a similar situation of struggling with heartache and loss, filled with questions and fears, overwhelmed by doubts and worries that left them lying awake at night, penned these simple words about trusting in God, and waiting ... cradled in God's hope.

With shattered souls
and hearts hollowed by loneliness,
with knees numb from kneeling
at bedsides and empty chapels
and hands aching from holding tight
to others through the night,
with lips longing to sing
and minds empty of the words,
we wait, we wait, we wait
for you and the hope
you shape from your own
tears.

Thom M Shuman

Sixth Week of Lent, Saturday

Bible reading:

... 'See, we are going up to Jerusalem, and the Son of Man will be handed over to the chief priests and the scribes, and they will condemn him to death; then they will hand him over to the Gentiles; they will mock him, and spit upon him, and flog him, and kill him; and after three days he will rise again.'

Mark 10:33–34 (NRSV)

Reflection:

We all know that there are lots of different ways to understand Jesus' crucifixion and resurrection. So let's not waste paper and time debating them. Instead, I wonder what this reading tells us about how we treat people. Jesus was, after all, the Son of Man. God experienced what we experience. So what did Jesus experience, and how is Jesus' crucifixion and resurrection being re-enacted today?

1. Jesus was handed over to the people who held the social power.

2. They condemned him.

3. They handed him back so that people could mock him, spit upon him, flog him, and kill him.

4. He will rise again.

Jesus was handed over to the people who held the social power. Who holds the social power today? I would suggest that power is held by our politicians and our media. They are the chief priests and scribes of today. The examples that they give us directly impact on how people live in this world. Shouting and braying in Parliament, prime ministers speaking hatefully about minorities, media outlets giving voices to homophobes, trans-sceptics and racists. These are the horrific indicators of social power today.

They condemned him. So who exactly do those who hold social power condemn today? I would suggest that they condemn 'the others'. Those who are poor, black, brown, disabled, LGBTQ+, foreign; and those who speak the truth to power when that truth supports 'the other'. Poor people are condemned for how they choose to spend the little money that they have. Black and brown people are condemned, and even killed, simply for daring to walk the streets of cities and towns. Disabled people are condemned for asking that places and events be made accessible. LGBTQ+ people are condemned for existing. Foreign people are condemned for having the courage to start a new life in this strange country.

They handed him back so that people could mock him, spit upon him, flog him, and kill him. And so it is today. Every day people in the UK are harassed, assaulted, abused, and even killed, simply for daring to be 'different'. Hate crimes, crimes committed because of someone's perceived differences, are becoming ever more common. It is becoming dangerous to be different. It is even becoming risky to speak out for social justice. But it is not simply those who commit these crimes who are to blame. Those who hold social power hand people over to those who wish to cause them pain by speaking carelessly. Every single wealthy, or white, or able-bodied, or heterosexual/cisgender, or British person has the power to choose their words. Please, please choose words of love and understanding. Don't hand people over to be crucified for their differences.

He will rise again. Jesus' resurrection shows us that this is not the end of the story. Like Jesus, the oppressed and marginalised will rise again. There is hope. But that hope is in our hands; it is in the stories that we tell. The witnesses to Jesus' resurrection enabled hope through the stories that they told. What story will you tell this Easter? I hope that it will be the story of resurrection: the story of accessibility, safety, diversity and justice. Witness the resurrection of the body of Christ, witness new life for all people.

Prayer:

In abundant mercy, hear our prayers.

God, you know what it feels like to tell friends frightening truths about yourself around a dinner table. We pray that our friends, our families and the churches to which we belong, or have left, or have been shut out of, might remember us as they remember you.

God, you know what it feels like to pray desperately for mercy whilst others sleep, ignorant of your fear and pain. We pray that people around the world might hear your call to stay awake – waking up to the injustice and oppression that we suffer, and speaking out for justice.

God, you know what it feels like to be betrayed, mocked and denied. We pray for those who have betrayed our identities, outed us, mocked us or denied our existence. May they recognise our existence and our humanity.

God, they called out for your crucifixion. And today, around the world, all sorts of people, some with worldly power, call out for our silencing and even our deaths. We pray for those who live under the threats of silence, abuse, violence and death.

Finally, God, we pray for all of those who have been buried in graves that bear names not their own. You call them by their name. You call us by our names.

We commit again to speaking up and acting out.

In the name of God, human, crucified, and yet bearing seemingly impossible hopes. Amen

Alex Clare-Young

Palm Sunday

Bible reading:

When they had come near Jerusalem and had reached Bethphage, at the Mount of Olives, Jesus sent two disciples, saying to them, 'Go into the village ahead of you, and immediately you will find a donkey tied, and a colt with her; untie them and bring them to me. If anyone says anything to you, just say this, "The Lord needs them." And he will send them immediately.' This took place to fulfil what had been spoken through the prophet, saying,

'Tell the daughter of Zion,
Look, your king is coming to you,
  humble, and mounted on a donkey,
    and on a colt, the foal of a donkey.'

The disciples went and did as Jesus had directed them; they brought the donkey and the colt, and put their cloaks on them, and he sat on them. A very large crowd spread their cloaks on the road, and others cut branches from the trees and spread them on the road. The crowds that went ahead of him and that followed were shouting,

'Hosanna to the Son of David!
  Blessed is the one who comes in the name of the Lord!
Hosanna in the highest heaven!'

When he entered Jerusalem, the whole city was in turmoil, asking, 'Who is this?' The crowds were saying, 'This is the prophet Jesus from Nazareth in Galilee.'

Matthew 21:1–11 (NRSV)

Reflection: Who is this?

Palm Sunday is often misunderstood. Sometimes referred to as a 'triumphal entry', or as a last moment of happiness before the darkness of Good Friday.

What is abundantly clear from Matthew's narrative is that Jesus had made careful preparations beforehand for this day and its consequences. No questions are asked of the two friends who use a kind of password in their request for the use of a donkey from local villagers. Then, there is the timing. Passover in Jerusalem was marked by tension, as thousands of pilgrims from the surrounding countryside and the Mediterranean world crowded into the city to celebrate the most important Jewish festival of the year, a time when, with nationalistic feelings running high, uprisings were always likely to break out. The authorities, both secular and religious, took no chances. Pontius Pilate, the Roman governor, resident in Jerusalem for Passover, drafted in extra military detachments to deal with any trouble.

The arrival of Jesus and his followers, from the Mount of Olives, would have been a kind of public demonstration and carefully watched by the security forces. The curious question reverberating round the crowded streets is a reminder that the Jesus movement was not widely known in Jerusalem and almost certainly not by international visitors. The reply to the question 'Who is this?' by those in the know is full of meaning. Every word is significant. This is Jesus, the prophet from Nazareth in Galilee. This is his name, this is his calling, this is where he comes from – an area notorious for unrest and insurrection. But this prophet comes in peace.

Those who knew scripture would remember that the prophets of Israel often used 'acted parables' in order to get their message across. They would recall Amos and his plumbline (Amos 7:8); Jeremiah's almond tree and a boiling cauldron over a fire (Jer 1:11–13), signs pointing to God's watchful judgement – dramatic actions which powerfully reinforced their spoken message. On this day they would call to mind the words of the prophet Zechariah:

… Lo, your king comes to you;
    triumphant and victorious is he,
humble and riding on a donkey,
    on a colt, the foal of a donkey.

He will cut off the chariot from Ephraim
   and the war-horse from Jerusalem;
and the battle bow shall be cut off,
   and he shall command peace to the nations …

(Zech 9:9–10, NRSV)

Jesus stands four-square in the succession of those remarkable 7th and 8th century BC characters who, with eloquence and imagination, spoke truth to power as God's word to an unjust society. As, with immense courage, Jesus begins the descent from the Mount of Olives into the heart of Jerusalem, he weeps over the city which will soon reject him and his message; in the name of the God of justice he challenges the corrupt Temple system which was robbing the poor, an action which inevitably sealed his fate.

Palm Sunday is supremely a time to reflect on the prophetic mission of Jesus and its relevance for today. The late John Hull never tired of reminding the church of its prophetic calling. He insisted that the training of priests, ministers and laity should contain not only theological understanding of the relevance of prophetic witness to the major social issues of our time, but its practical application in the political and economic marketplace. How seriously do we and the churches to which we belong take this call to prophetic vocation and action?

Prayer:

Jesus, prophet of God,
as we travel in your footsteps during this week
we ask for courage, imagination and compassion
in speaking truth to power
and in action for a more just, peaceful nation and world.
Amen

Warren Bardsley

Monday of Holy Week

Bible reading:

Mary took a pound of costly perfume made of pure nard, anointed Jesus' feet, and wiped them with her hair. The house was filled with the fragrance of the perfume.

John 12:3 (NRSV)

Reflection:

Have you ever done anything outrageous? Have you ever felt all eyes upon you? Have you ever wanted to show your love for someone? It was six days before the Passover, and Jesus had come to Bethany to the house I share with my sister Martha and my brother, Lazarus. It is evening, and I'm standing in the doorway, looking into the crowded room. I'm holding something precious, a flask of costly perfume, and I'm trying to gather my courage before it's too late. Martha is busy, serving the meal. We've spent all day preparing the food, and everyone is here, including the disciples, and our friends from the village. Lazarus is sitting at the table, full of life and laughing.

Now I come into the room and no one sees me. I carry my flask of perfume and I go straight up to the table. I kneel down and pour the perfume over Jesus' feet. Then I wipe his feet with my hair. The talking stops, and all eyes look at me: shocked eyes, astonished eyes, fearful eyes. Only Judas is scornful: 'Why was this perfume not sold for three hundred denarii and the money given to the poor?' I stare at him. Who are you to sneer? This is my house. This is my perfume. You are here as a guest and you are eating food that I have prepared. Who are you to judge?

Jesus is looking at me as if he sees into my heart. He is the one who defends me. He says that I've kept the perfume for the day of his burial. He tells us all that we will always have the poor with us but we will not always have him. But I hadn't bought the perfume for his burial. I don't want him to die. I want to thank him for what he has done for us. He has given Lazarus life. I want to give him a gift now. I want to make the most of this moment while he is here with us. I don't want to think of the future. I don't want to think about what might happen to him in Jerusalem. I start to pray: *Don't let it be soon. Don't let it happen. Let us just be in this moment.*

The scent of the perfume begins to spread through the house. We all breathe in the rich and powerful scent. They start to eat again and talk again, and I sit down at the table. The scent is reassuring – it takes away my fears. It holds a promise of good days to come, days of joy and peace. My perfume is not to be sold to the rich. It's for all of us. I look round the faces at the table: old friends and new. I see the widow who lost her home, the woman who had no food, and the man who used to sit and beg. Some people are talking about the ways to change society, to make sure that everyone has a home, and everyone has food. We need to find a new way of living so that everyone can have a good life. Jesus and the disciples are talking about the festival of Passover in Jerusalem. Lazarus wants to go up this year. He wants us all to go up to celebrate the feast with Jesus. He wants to be with Jesus when he enters the city with his crowds of followers.

The moment has passed – but that moment hasn't gone. It will stay with me always. I know that Jesus is the Messiah, the Anointed One. I anointed him that evening – it was me not a prophet or a priest. I didn't anoint his head as king – but I did anoint his feet because he walks the costly path of peace.

The moment has passed, and Jesus is no longer in our house but the scent of the perfume reminds me of that evening – and I know that he is with us always. I'm glad I took the risk. I brought Jesus my gift of costly perfume. I anointed his feet and wiped them with my hair. Have you ever done any-thing outrageous? Have you ever felt all eyes upon you? Have you ever wanted to show your love for someone?

On Monday evening
it's time to rest
to share a meal with friends
for the hour draws near
and the path is becoming narrow.
It's time to remember Mary of Bethany
and her gift of costly perfume
which spread through the house.
Six days before the Passover
as Jesus journeyed to Jerusalem.

Susan Miller

Tuesday of Holy Week

Bible readings:

> … *do not forsake me when my strength is spent.*
> *For my enemies speak concerning me,*
>   *and those who watch for my life consult together.*
> *They say, 'Pursue and seize that person*
>   *whom God has forsaken,*
>   *for there is no one to deliver.'*
>
> *O God, do not be far from me.*
>   *O my God, make haste to help me!*

Psalm 71:9b–12 (NRSV)

> *'Very truly, I tell you, unless a grain of wheat falls into the earth and dies, it remains just a single grain; but if it dies, it bears much fruit.'*

John 12:24 (NRSV)

Reflection:

We all have experiences from long ago that pop back into our mind from time to time. Let me share two.

First one: fifty years ago! Driving to Accrington on a hospital visit I noticed the sky turning unusually dark. Street lights were coming on; car lights; house lights. Within minutes, early afternoon had become midnight. No eclipse I have experienced has ever so effectively extinguished all signs of natural light.

I parked opposite the entrance and waited. Everything was waiting. There was an eerie silence. At last a line of grey light appeared, stretching the entire horizon – growing as the end of the cloud silently approached and slowly passed overhead. Daylight was back. Then, without warning, the storm broke – a curtain of water, blotting out the hospital, cascading down the road. Only when I thought it was easing did I risk a dash to the entrance, and squelched down the corridor.

There was a strange atmosphere in the wards. Nurses seemed distracted. The person I had come to see told me some of them had been praying. 'They thought the end of the world had come,' she said. Next day, newspapers reported that the cloud was a mile thick.

Second one: Holy Week on Iona, called 'Experiencing Easter': twenty-five years ago.

We were guests at the Abbey, and as the drama unfolded I felt it was happening to me. In a sense, it was – changing for ever the way I relate to Holy Week. I longed for folk back home to feel it too. But back home we come to church for fragments of the narrative – Palm Sunday service, Maundy Thursday meal, Good Friday walk, Easter morning Eucharist. On Iona we had lived it, as the days built to a crescendo.

Sheila and I have since gone through three more of these weeks, as members of staff. Always powerful, though not quite the same when you're working there. Distractions would catch us unawares; minor irritations explode into major issues. Why, on this of all weeks? Perhaps we were torn between our duties and wanting to participate. Maybe it was too near the beginning of the season for things to run smoothly yet.

But I have my own theory: that unconsciously we were suffering from grief. We could feel the weekend looming: an intimate supper to be sabotaged by betrayal; an Abbey Church to be stripped and darkened. No singing in church the next day; just an empty cross hanging there in all its starkness. And on the Saturday, after the busyness and excitement of the week – nothing. I used to say to myself, and to others working there: 'Don't rise to petty disputes and complaints; they are most likely about something else; we're all out of sorts this week. Wait till Sunday.'

Easter Sunday on Iona was quite something. A guest told me that trouble weighing on her all week, all year in fact, vanished for good when she turned and saw that cross come through the door of the church, transformed, decked with flowers.

So if we know the outcome of the story, why should grief overshadow the week? Why? – because light cannot break though the darkness if there is no darkness. We can only identify deeply with the story by experiencing the depths, as if we do not know how it will end. A grain must die and fall in the ground if it is to bear fruit.

Prayer:

When did you first see it, Lord –
that darkening horizon?
How long did you keep it to yourself
before you began to tell us
what would be awaiting you in Jerusalem?
We didn't take it in then,
and made no sense at all of your postscript about the third day.
Nonetheless, we who had been so eager to follow you
started hanging back;
had to be dragged along like stubborn mules.

So our noisy arrival was all bravado …
you on that bewildered donkey,
us shouting and cheering,
waving branches, carpeting the road with our clothes,
mocking Pontius Pilate's pompous entry last week
… all bravado on our part, Lord.
Storm clouds were building; no mistaking them now.

Yet still you carry on
as if this is your moment in the sun –
disrupting the temple, goading the authorities.
Only those nearest to you heard the words you used
to excuse that Mary girl for washing your feet with perfume.

Only you and your dearest companions, it seems,
have noticed the daylight fading.

But soon all will see:
see that nothing can be seen.
Thick darkness,
like the end of the world.

Then the storm!
Everything falling apart –
your friends run for cover,
your following disperses,
your faith cracks …
… before the break of day.

> Stay by me, Lord,
> when I fail to stay by you.
> Pray forgiveness for me,
> for I know not what I do.
> God in my emptiness,
> Christ in my brokenness,
> Light in my darkest hour,
> bring me back to you.

Brian Woodcock

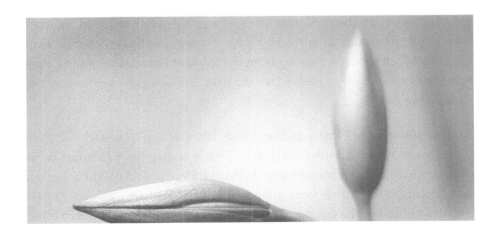

Wednesday of Holy Week

Bible reading:

… Let us run with perseverance the race that is set before us, looking to Jesus the pioneer and perfecter of our faith, who for the sake of the joy that was set before him endured the cross …

Consider him who endured such hostility against himself from sinners, so that you may not grow weary or lose heart.

Hebrews 12:1b–2a, 3 (NRSV)

Reflection:

When I was young, decades ago, we sang a chorus about following Jesus which ended with the phrase 'No turning back, no turning back'. In the middle of Holy Week, in the middle of the Passion story, there can be no turning back for Jesus. The Cross is already looming; the hostility toward him is growing. But for his followers, hard choices remain. Stay the course or disappear into the crowd? How would we make that decision today?

We shouldn't dismiss how uncomfortable that choice is, even now. The Cross is a disturbing reality at the heart of our faith in Christ. It speaks of pain and rejection; betrayal and loss – things we prefer to avoid. When I served in congregational ministry, I noticed many faithful folk would skip the Holy Week services, moving from the jubilant Procession of the Palms one Sunday to the joy of Easter Day the next. We will close our eyes to the Cross if we can.

And yet some forms of pain and rejection, betrayal and loss mark our lives too. This is true for individuals. It is also a reality for Christian communities in different places around the world. Here in Canada the rejection and hostility the Church faces arise mostly from our own failures in past decades to live out the Gospel in humane and hospitable ways. But in other contexts, churches as well as other religious communities face deadlier forms of oppression, which means Hebrews' call for perseverance also demands courage and sacrifice.

When I worked at the MacLeod Centre on Iona, such courage and sacrifice became palpable the week we welcomed asylum seekers and their community advocates. It was an eclectic international group including several people who had faced religious persecution – Christians, Muslims and a secular Jewish family. Their stories inspired respect and compassion. One conversation I'll never forget. We asked our guests about the role music played in their spirituality and if it helped them face the oppression they'd had to flee. Both the Muslims and the Jews spoke about lament, and the ways in which music allowed them to release their prayer and pain to the Holy One. The Christians, mainly from African contexts, offered a different perspective. They talked about 'singing the devil down'. For them singing songs of faith increased their strength and courage, and moved them to active resistance. It was quite a conversation.

In the middle of Holy Week, the music of our faith turns my eyes toward Jesus again and again. I resonate with the haunting laments, set in the mystery of minor keys, which sing about pain and betrayal. I sing out memories of my own pain even while I confess the betrayal of the Gospel I have been party to. My favourite song for the middle of Holy Week is 'What wondrous love is this'. This old American folk tune starts each verse with a haunting ache, but then soaring hope emerges as the melody moves along. While I might not call this 'singing the devil down', I find the gift of this music is the gift Hebrews promises – that we will not grow weary or lose heart in the middle of Holy Week, as the shadows around Jesus deepen.

This old tune and its lyrics bring me comfort and encouragement at other times too. The music travels with me through loss or heartache, giving voice to my yearning – and to the faith that gives me strength. It reminds me to 'look to Jesus' in those moments, telling me I am not alone. And that's why our reflections during Holy Week are so important. The stories, the music, the prayers tell us we are not alone when pain and rejection, betrayal or loss catch us up. Such times often make us long to turn back – from life and perhaps also from our faith – to regain happier, more positive moods and hope that is less tangled up with complexity. We need the encouragement Hebrews repeats so that even if we do grow weary, we will not lose heart.

Holy Week is full of complexity, for Jesus and for his followers, then and now. Thank God that for Jesus, there was no turning back. For when we are tripped up by life, we know that Jesus is with us. He has been through the sorrows we face – and more. Marking the footsteps of Jesus this week tells us not only what Jesus did for us but that Jesus goes with us. So let the music of this season sing with you and through you this week, to claim this truth and fill your heart with both the courage and consolation Jesus offers.

A spiritual practice for today:

Recall your favourite hymn or music written for Holy Week. Hum or sing the tune throughout this day. Let the music release to God any heartache you are carrying. Let the melody surround you with a sense of God's encouragement. Use the words of the hymn to lead you in prayer and reflection, looking to Jesus as your constant companion in your journey, just as you join him in his.

Nancy Cocks

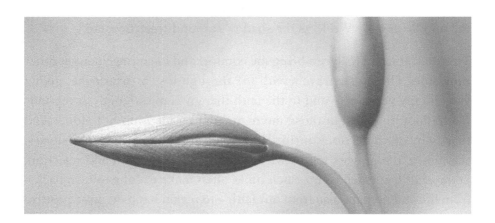

Maundy Thursday

Bible reading:

Then he poured water into a basin and began to wash the disciples' feet and to wipe them with the towel that was tied around him. He came to Simon Peter, who said to him, 'Lord, are you going to wash my feet?' Jesus answered, 'You do not know now what I am doing, but later you will understand.' Simon Peter said to him, 'You will never wash my feet.' Jesus answered, 'Unless I wash you, you have no share with me.' Simon Peter said to him, 'Lord not my feet only but also my hands and my head!'

John 13:5–9 (NRSV)

Reflection: Eucharistic living

Who washes your feet?

Between my three spinal operations, Sue, one of my former students, offered to massage my feet. I accepted with reluctance and some embarrassment but am so grateful that I did. Reflexology is an alternative medicine and involves bringing pressure to the hands and feet with thumb and finger techniques. Later I learned that the massaging of feet can increase bowel movement.

In the story of Jesus washing the feet of his disciples, and Simon Peter's difficulty in accepting this, Jesus says, 'If you are not able to receive, you can no longer be a disciple of mine.' Openness to receiving the gifts of God through encounters which may threaten us brings the possibility of transformation, as Simon Peter discovered in his encounter with the Gentile Cornelius (Acts 10:1–48), and as Jesus discovered with the Samaritan woman at the well (Jn 4:1–15).

Bill Watty was a former President of the Methodist Church in the Caribbean. His searing words, written in the 1960s, still stir my soul. 'Can a missionary-minded Church receive?' he wrote. And his conclusion? 'No, a missionary-minded Church can only give – and hence its soul is in peril.'

With others I was taught, as a young Christian, how to open my hands in order to receive bread in Communion; how to stretch out my hands for the cup. 'Live with open hands,' we were taught. 'Closed hands can receive nothing.'

I was not familiar with the phrase 'Eucharistic living' until I met Michael Wilson in the final years of his life. He had been a doctor in Ghana, a priest at St-Martin-in-the-Fields in London and Director of the Pastoral Studies Department in Birmingham University. He lived with a huge fungating cancerous lump on his neck. He invited me to be his 'Eucharistic person'. I quickly learned that the invitation was much more than a prearranged devotional sacramental slot on a Thursday afternoon. Michael was much more interested in what he called 'Eucharistic living' than Eucharistic liturgies.

Eucharistic living is about being open to receiving the gifts of God through dark and light, through the creative and destructive, through the essential otherness of those who are different. We explored what it could mean to lay ourselves open to receive the gifts of God through people of the different world faith communities, different sexual orientations, different cultural backgrounds – to receive and to lay ourselves open to the possibility of transformation. In the Eucharist we say: God gives God's very self within the membranes of life and draws us into the mystery of providing within unexpected ways and unexpected places.

Eucharistic living is about being open to receiving, and it is also about experiencing and expressing gratitude. Old Cyril in Notting Hill, on receiving bread in Communion, murmured not a pious 'Amen' but a shrill 'thank you!' – a thank you for God's goodness in circumstances that most of us would find it hard to bear.

On some occasions when I visited Michael on a Thursday afternoon there was the smell of freshly baked bread made by his wife, Jean. Often he greeted me from his chair with 'Come and see' – and led me into the garden to look at some shrub, plant, flower or bush. He found immense joy and wonder in creation. He said once: 'When we arrive at the gates of heaven we will be asked one question: "Have you found delight in my creation and delight in each other?'" Over and over again Michael reminded me that it is God's intention that we find joy in each other.

Eucharistic living is about sharing. Perhaps you also are shaken by the sight of aid workers throwing bread into the outstretched hands of girls and boys, women and men in refugee camps. Perhaps you also are impatient with the Church's Eucharistic practice that individualises, privatises, spiritualises and institutionalises the bread-sharing of Jesus among the people. I wish that Michael had lived to hear of the Bread Church in Liverpool, where all sorts and conditions of people, including asylum seekers and *Big Issue* sellers, made bread together – two loaves: one to keep and the other to give away. Together they explored the mystery of yeast, of kneading and rising within their own stories and the stories of their communities. Companions – we are learning – are those who share with us the bread of life.

Father Tissa Balasuriya, a Roman Catholic priest from Sri Lanka, on a visit to Birmingham, spoke of a billion Eucharists taking place where Christians share bread but still refuse to share their bread in the world. 'Perhaps we need to call a moratorium on Eucharists until we come to share our bread with the world's hungry and thirsty. How can our Eucharists become a sign of real sharing in the world?' he asked.

To ponder:

Who washes your feet? …

Prayer:

God, enable us to trust in your holding, unfolding and withholding hand.
Enable us to receive the gifts that come in both joy and grief.
Enable us to receive what you promise to be necessary
for the living of each day.

Donald Eadie

Good Friday

Bible reading:

He was despised and rejected by others;
a man of suffering and acquainted with infirmity …
The NAME took pleasure in …
the one who made his life an offering for sin (asham) …
He bore the sins of many
and made intercession for the transgressors.

Isaiah 53:3,10,12 (NRSV, amended)

Reflection:

Many cultures and political dynasties have understood themselves in terms of a myth of election: God has chosen me, or this nation, to carry out God's purposes. One expression of it in Scripture is the royal ideology of David and Jerusalem. The collapse of Judah in 586 BC and the end of the Davidic dynasty called this into question. Did this mean that the NAME, the God Israel worshipped, became a nothing, a mere historical referent, like the gods of Assyria?

The prophets of the exile and the editors of the Torah address this question. The most astonishing response comes from the person or persons who wrote the four so-called 'servant songs' of Second Isaiah, and especially whoever it was who wrote the fourth song, the reading for today. This poet inverted the old Davidic ideology. The royal ideology fawned and spluttered before the king: he was 'God's son', a priest king, God would always protect him (Ps 45). His beauty is a sign that God has chosen him (1 Sam 16:12). 'God', here, is effectively the tribal fetish of Judah, the social identity of Judah and the Davidic dynasty deified. The poet of the servant songs sees that this idea is idolatrous. The first three servant songs abandon royal sycophancy and see election in terms of service – a very radical idea.

There's no agreement, of course, about what the historical Jesus actually said, but it's pretty sure that he made servanthood a defining characteristic of his self-understanding (Mk 10:45). Where did he get that idea from? Paul, in one of his great hymns, understands Jesus as a servant, or slave, and understands Christian existence accordingly (Phil 2:5–11). It beggars belief that Jesus and/or the early community had not ruminated on the servant texts in Isaiah.

The poet of the fourth song goes further. Unlike David, the servant has no beauty, is despised, humiliated, tortured, imprisoned, buried with offenders (this later becomes the structure of the creed: born, suffered, died, was buried). Paul and the author of Hebrews understand this humiliation in terms of the shame of the cross (1 Cor 1:25, Gal 3:13, Phil 2:7, Heb 12:2) and like the poet of the exile they understand it as part of the structure of salvation. The poet only hints at vindication (v.10); for the Messianic community shame exists dialectically with exaltation.

Four things are going on in the poem. First, and most importantly, in redefining election, the poet redefines how we are to understand 'God'. 'God' is not that which underwrites social hierarchy and the existing property order. The NAME is not a monarch writ large, but seen and known in the humiliated and despised. This is why we speak of 'revelation': we are told what we cannot tell ourselves.

Bound up with this is the very profound idea (explored by Iris Murdoch in *The Unicorn*) that God, or the good, is non-powerful – saves by refusing to pass suffering on. Even suffering can be powerful (Dostoevsky has a lot to say about this). Our poet sees that the NAME refuses even this power. The NAME bears evil, forgives it, puts an end to it by refusing the response which is part of the endless cycle of violence. Jesus' words on not resisting evil represent a profound reflection on the ideas of the fourth song.

When the poet wrote, the temple lay in ruins, and there was no sacrificial cultus. People wanted it back, and under Nehemiah they got it back, prioritising what had earlier been the least significant part of sacrifice, the guilt offering. Later the church did exactly the same thing in the sacrifice of the Mass. The dynamics of guilt cry out for sacrificial ritual. The poet of the fourth song is leery of this idea. We do not need it. In the life of this humiliated one the *asham*, the guilt offering, has been offered once and for all. Sacrifice is radically desacralised. The author of Hebrews puts this end of sacrifice at the heart of his understanding of the life of faith. All that remains is the sacrifice of praise (Heb 13:7) and the concrete act of witness and confession of faith, as well as a service of love (13:15) – an idea we find in Paul as well (Rom 12:1, Phil 2:17).

Underpinning the fourth song is what was later called the idea of vicariousness. The poet understands that each is bound up with the life of all. ('To all am I bounden', says Edwin Muir.)[1] Whether we know it or not, or like it or not, we live for and from others. In the servant, according to the poet, and in Jesus, according to the Messianic writings, this is recognised and taken up as a signal of the NAME'S relationship to all people and all things. In them the vicariousness of all life is visceral.

Ave crux, unica spes ('Hail, O cross, our only hope'). Why? Because the cross frees us from the god of projection, the god of our internalised guilty conscience who wants to flog us before forgiving us. It frees us from what the author(s) of Ephesians and Colossians call the 'powers', who whisper in our ear that we can only be saved by power, greatness and violence. It frees us for the sacrifice of praise, which is a life coming out of thankfulness and going back to it – what our tradition calls the life of grace. In these two liberations it addresses our 'sin', our enslavement to the powers, our turned inwardness, magnified by the turned inwardness of our group, culture or nation. As Paul and John note, it is a call to freedom (2 Cor 3:17, Gal 5:1, Jn 8:36).

Prayer:

Lord God,
you give yourself to be known
in the humiliation of the cross.
Free us from our idolatries
as you have freed us from the fear of death.
Help us to follow you in
service.

Timothy Gorringe

Note:

1. From 'The debtor', by Edwin Muir

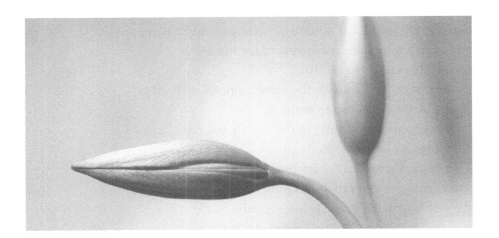

Holy Saturday

Bible reading:

When it was evening, there came a rich man from Arimathea, named Joseph, who was also a disciple of Jesus. He went to Pilate and asked for the body of Jesus; then Pilate ordered it to be given to him. So Joseph took the body and wrapped it in a clean linen cloth and laid it in his own new tomb, which he had hewn in the rock. He then rolled a great stone to the door of the tomb and went away. Mary Magdalene and the other Mary were there, sitting opposite the tomb.

Matthew 27:57–61 (NRSV)

Reflection:

Sitting opposite the tomb
a rich man:
doubly rich for he has a place of belonging and a name,
and even a tomb, already prepared for his death
(death that comes to us all).
Two women, blessed with the same name as each other,
sisters in sorrow, who are not rich:
they have lost everything, in the one they loved.
Now they sit opposite the tomb.
There's another man, Nicodemus,
sometimes the story includes him,
the one who went to see Jesus, secretly, by night,
seeking, reasoning, arguing about the truth.
He's the one who was challenged to be born again;
he comes back, again at night,
because of death, not birth, to help bury Jesus.
This is the hard truth now.
Everything is back to front: a tomb for a womb.
Just like other wise men, Nicodemus brings a gift:
spices, bitter myrrh and aloes, for embalming.
The spices are heavy.

The body is a dead weight.
The stone to seal the tomb is heavy.
The women are empty-handed
as they sit opposite the tomb.
Two men ... a corpse ... a linen shroud ... a rock-hewn tomb
    ... a great stone
two women
sitting, waiting, watching the tomb.
What are they waiting for?
They waited while he was dying, when the men had run away.
They kept faith.
The death they witnessed was ugly, agonising,
sweat and blood, gasping breaths and cries of despair.
Now everything is calm.
They did what they could when the men had carried him there.
They saw his eyes were closed,
they folded his wounded body in the clean cloth,
there was safe cradling in the limestone cave.
They heard the stone rumble into place.
Silence.
What are they waiting for?
Death will come to us all. This is not about fear.
There are things to be done, decencies to observe.
Busyness, then numbness.
The words will come later:
Silence and emptiness now,
being present to an absence.
So, with no grounds for hope, they keep faith.
The women sit opposite the tomb:
confronting this death with steadfast love.

Reflect on your own experience of dealing with death: how you coped (or
have seen others cope) with 'doing what needs to be done' before the
funeral; how important it is not to hide in busyness, or too many words;
to seek silence, to keep faith, even when you cannot pray.

Jan Sutch Pickard

Easter Sunday

Bible reading:

'for you have died, and your life is hidden with Christ in God'.

Colossians 3:3 (NRSV)

Reflection:

Though I love the Easter resurrection stories, and have preached about them often, it is many years since I understood them as being about the resuscitation of corpses, my own or anyone else's, or about what will happen to me when I'm dead – if indeed, I ever thought about them that way. Of course, they involve death and bodies and touch. But they are stories about life. And they are strange and mysterious stories indeed.

The least strange thing in Holy Week is the crucifixion. It is the most wearily predictable thing in the whole story, the familiar memory of suffering, undeserved and unjustifiable. But the resurrection is exceedingly strange. All the post-resurrection narratives emphasise its strangeness; all these meetings with friends who don't recognise Jesus, all the intimations of a strange new way of being in relationship, which underline a break from the past; 'do not try to hold on to me'. But also, in all these stories of strangeness, the refrain, 'do not be afraid'.

'What do these stories mean?' is a question to which many answers have been suggested over the centuries, and to which, truthfully, I have nothing to add. But if I ask instead, 'what do these stories mean to me; are they still a story to live by for me?', I know that here is something that is absolutely a reality in my living of my life. And yet it is almost too deep to express, except in occasional words and phrases, or in poetry.

This verse from Colossians speaks to my condition. I remember that George MacLeod often quoted it, and wrote about it in *We Shall Rebuild*: *'It means that so far as we are concerned the undertaker has been and gone; it is a matter of indifference to us whether at some future date anyone will or will not put a wreath of flowers on the box that contains our mortal remains.'*

It's a strange metaphor. It has intimations of freedom, the 'do not be afraid', of letting go of what we don't need to carry, and of what Thomas Merton called *'the surrender of the deep will'*. It's about not living accommodated to a death-dealing world order. It's about the choice to live. Life is what we have, life is the gift. I am in love with the Life of life. So it's also a decision to live hopefully. And to be part of a community of hope, with everyone who bears daily witness that the last word is the Life of life, is to trust that in the embracing of the reality of death, there is a gift of enormous agency, a power of love stronger than death, a possibility for transformation. And at the heart of our life as a community of love is gratitude, the amazed wonder that it is indeed so, the 'being-in-love' that is a response to experiencing the ground of our being as, beyond everything, grace.

Or perhaps it's simply another way of giving yourself up to the sea.

When you're in the sea
and it's very dark
and very stormy
and very cold
and actually, you think you're drowning
and you're very scared
and you see a piece of wood
drifting by in the middle distance
you don't hang around to ask questions
or to speculate about how it got there
and why
and who sent it.
You just swim as hard as you can towards it
and you grab it
and cling on for dear life.

In the back of your mind you know
it's not a boat

and it will not give you
either direction
or control.
You're still at the mercy of the flood tide
and whether you like it or not
you're going where it takes you.
But to be honest
you don't care.
You just want not to drown.
And the wood offers hope
support
a bit of respite for your aching arms and back
a feeling of not being completely abandoned
something solid to hold on to in the
midst of all this insubstantial water and dark and wind
and stop you panicking.
A way to give yourself up to the sea.

I haven't reached dry land yet
but I'm in sight of the shore.
The piece of wood is still with me
and it's funny
but I've got to kind of like being in the water.

Of course, it's easier to say that
when you can see land!

Prayer:

Christ our life,
You are alive in the beauty of the earth
in the rhythm of the seasons
in the mystery of time and space.
ALLELUIA

Christ our life,
You are alive in the tenderness of touch
in the heartbeat of intimacy
in the insights of solitude.
ALLELUIA

Christ our life,
You are alive in the creative possibility
of the dullest conversation
the dreariest task
the most nerve-racking event.
ALLELUIA

Christ our life,
You are alive to offer new creation
to every unhealed hurt
to every deadened place
to every damaged heart.
ALLELUIA

You set before us a great choice.
Therefore we choose life.
ALLELUIA

Kathy Galloway

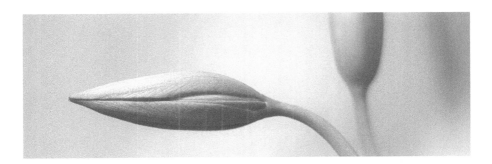

More resources for
Lent, Holy Week
and Easter

Lent

The temptation sonnets

The stone (Matthew 4:1–4)

I am the stone which, had he so chosen,
would, at his command, have changed into bread;
satisfied hunger, though far from ambrosian:
forty days banished of going unfed.
I know I was tempting, my colour, my shape,
lying nearby and so easy to grasp;
I swear that his mouth was just briefly agape
as he visualised eating me, his voice a harsh rasp.

It would have been weird to be what I'm not;
stone is my nature and stone I remain.
To change me to bread would have robbed me of what
is truly myself, my self would be slain.
He resisted; respected my right to be stone,
and that all I require is to be left alone.

The pinnacle of the Temple (Matthew 4:5–7)

Why pick on me? My role has always been
to support the priest, quite literally, each day
as dawn approaches; from me he's clearly seen
to signal-start the sacrifice. You say
mine is a modest role? Perhaps, but where,
if not on me, would you suggest he stand?
The priest, I mean. The sacrifice, the prayer,
the daily Temple practice as Yahweh planned.

When he, the desert man, was lifted here
(as if he were the highest of High Priests),
what next? Self-sacrifice? The drop is sheer!

Then angel-borne? Or carrion for the beasts?
I was relieved by his refusal, elated,
lest in his downfall I'd be implicated.

The mountain (Matthew 4:8–11)

Strictly speaking, I'm not quite high enough
to be called a mountain, more like a hill;
though, true, you can see the countryside and stuff
spread out at my foot. It was quite a thrill
when I was chosen as the very spot
from which to view the kingdoms of the earth,
though once again in truth there's not a lot:
just the Roman one for what that's worth.

I've gathered, though, that there are many more
which he then scrutinised with inward eye;
yet he's decided to ignore (ignore!)
the power and glory he's been offered. Why?
I'd like to be the highest mountain, such
that you'd look up to me. That's not asking much.

Richard Skinner

Temptations

As he slumped in the shop doorway,
grubby sleeping bag drawn up to his chin,
the voice whispered:
'There's an empty pizza box in that waste bin.
If you really are who you claim to be
put a pizza in it.
The sort you like –
deep-pan with cheese, olives and tomatoes.'
He shook his head.
'Food isn't enough,'
he muttered.

As he stumbled through the rain towards the church porch,
he looked up at the spire.
And the voice spoke again:
'Get up there and jump.
You'd be kept safe.
What a sensation that would be –
they'd all listen to you then.'
He hissed through clenched teeth
'I will not ... I must not ...
tempt God.'

As he sank down onto the cold floor of the stairwell
of the multi-storey car park,
he heard:
'Why are you here?
This isn't the way.
Become a celeb,
write your memoirs,
get on TV,
become a politician,
a business tycoon –
make a killing.
You could get right to the top,
if you follow my advice:
do things my way.'
'God alone is my master,'
he said.
'I'll serve Him,
and only Him.'
The voice departed,
and the angels came.

Brian Ford

Cold hours

Lent, for me, is always an experience of failure.
Or perhaps it is simply disillusionment.

I start with
    fire kindled by ashes,
    passion for passion,
    and readiness for transformation.

I set aside time,
    and step into emptiness,
    believing.

But the weeks are long,
    and the waiting
    falters in the cold hours,
    when doubt clings damply
    to the bones.

Then the gap between who I am,
    and who I dream of being,
    is revealed again.

I am like the dead who lie silent,
    waiting for resurrection,
    some anxiously, some confidently,
    and for me, a bit of both.

Perhaps those cold hours with the dead
are what it's all about.

Tony McClelland

Wilderness ...

... an outside nothing-space
where rock and shrub and stone
preside.

A lonely-presence place
where fears confront
and devils tempt.

Our care-filled
lifetime's skill
of busy occupation
too easily steps aside
from wilderness,
from silence,
so from the
deeper places of the soul,
we hide.

Lenten wilderness beckons us
to pause awhile,
and there to find
attending angels
holding us with Christ.

Engaging Lent re-calls us.

In his presence
from hill and plain
we reach
a borrowed room,
a carried cross,
and then
a garden meeting-place
of rock and shrub and stone,
dawn-kissed,
and touched by grace.

Stephen J Maunder

Floral tribute

Can flowers speak?
They spoke to me in church
at Passiontide.

From an earthen vase
on a table of smooth, light wood
carved with the words:
'Do this in remembrance of me'
I heard purple irises,
their spear-shaped open petals
whispering of the sacrifice
of their dying Lord;
the crowding greenery –
like prickly privet bristles –
cry of his crown of thorns;
and, underneath them all,
in humble joy, the bursting,
golden daffodils'
Resurrection trumpets
silently announcing that life
lives on, through death.

Carol Dixon

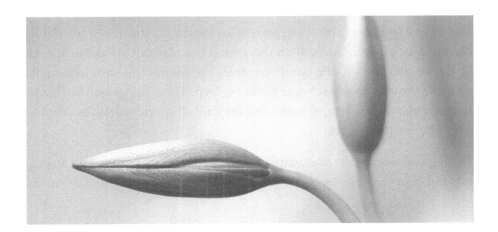

Holy Week

Coping

Written in October 2016, just before the election of Donald Trump

Bible reading: Matthew 21:12–13

I started this reflection before the election in the USA. It was sent to *Coracle,* the magazine of the Iona Community, before we knew very much about what the regime change in Washington would actually look like. But now I know. I am frightened; it seems a different world. I need comfort more than ever. But the mountains rising behind our farm fields haven't moved. And I know that for the time being, the tamaracks glowing their autumn yellow will drop their needles and come green again in the spring. Green is hopeful.

It is early morning. I sit on a dock by the side of a lake in the middle of the Adirondack Mountains of New York. I do not need to pray, for it is all prayer: my presence, the gentle breezes scurrying across the surface, the tall sentinel pines emerging over the deciduous canopy. If I am lucky, a loon will call, with a voice as ethereal as a moonbeam. I am never closer to God than when I am here. I breathe in grace and breathe out praise and gratitude.

There is a set of cabins behind me, built by my grandfather over a century ago. I am deeply grateful to him. With careful maintenance, this camp may endure for another hundred years for our family.

I smile and feel joy at that. But this is what breaks my heart: my grandchildren may not hear a loon call on this lake. They may not see the brilliance of red maples in autumn, nor even smell the fragrant balsam fir boughs that line the lean-to where we sometimes sleep. These things will be chased northward by rising temperatures, for they are all species carefully adapted to cooler northern forests.

During the coming decades, earthly changes will result in massive migrations of people, millions of deaths and extinctions of many species. It has already begun. I despair, and fear deeply for my grandchildren, but even more for other people's grandchildren residing in more vulnerable regions of the earth.

At times my despair and fear overwhelms me. But three mutually supporting, intricately connected webs sustain me and help me cope.

First is an *intimacy* I feel with the crazy, beautiful, infinitely varied and wildly intricate other-than-human world.

This intimacy is a journey that began when I was very small, walking in the woods with my parents in the spring, searching for the first funky spears of skunk cabbage. Over my childhood years, I was blessed to grow up with marshes, woods, fields, ponds and streams nearby and to encounter all their varied inhabitants as familiar friends. My husband and I now live in a house full of windows offering expansively exquisite views across farm fields reaching toward mountains to the west. The sunsets sometimes cause us to just wait and watch in wonder. At night, the skies are dark, the Milky Way clearly visible. In the winter, I can trace Orion's journey across the night skies.

My intimacy with the natural world was enriched by academic ecological studies. For instance, I can read about a 'trophic cascade' in Yellowstone Park and understand the dynamics: reintroduced predator wolves keep elk populations in check; streamside alders are browsed less; waters cool; and fish flourish. All things are connected. My mind bursts with wonder and my heart is deeply moved by the science and the story of it all. I feel gratitude to the scientists who discover and document these relationships through years of careful study, and to the ecosystems that can and will adapt in their own ways to changes. Adapting means enduring, and that brings hope.

The second web supporting me is my *faith*. Scientists tell us the most fundamental things are outside space and time; I call these God. The marvels of evolution; the collective witness, wisdom and experiences of many faiths; and chaos theory, among other things, are all evidence for God's existence.

My own experience of God seals my belief. I was brought up in a liberal religious tradition. There is no dogma associated with the word 'God' for me.

God is not an all-powerful, patriarchal, judgemental, punishing arbiter of right and wrong. Rather, as Rabbi Michael Lerner has said, *'God is also all that makes possible the transformation from "that which* is*" to "that which can and* ought *to be"'* (my emphases).[1] To me, God is not supernatural, but wholly natural, in relationship, a shared experience. Through unconditional love, God is forever becoming, always transforming the past into the present to make the future, offering opportunities, while leaving freedom to choose. God, in other words, is both self-limiting and, as one denomination so eloquently puts it, *'still speaking'*. Part of what God has to say can be seen in the processes and intricacies of earth systems. They are therefore sacred.

So for me, the presence of the divine in my life is ubiquitous, familiar, inspiring and comforting. Never negative, never judging and never remote. (If at certain points I do not feel the presence of God, the limitation is at my end.)

The third web supporting me, in the face of climate change, is the broad *community* of people dedicated to social and environmental justice.

Climate change has enhanced our understanding of the evils of injustice to the poor. For example, when oil train cars – daily arriving in Albany, New York with their highly volatile cargo from North Dakota – are vented in the summer heat directly alongside the bedrooms of children in affordable housing sections of the city, causing grave sickness and maybe even death, everyone should shriek in opposition. But most do not, despite knowing that this is one of millions of instances where our addiction to fossil fuels hurts human beings and others.

Some people do shriek, though, and object and lobby and march and commit acts of civil disobedience. Just as I feel support though my love of the wild world and of God, I gain support from knowing there are like-minded people speaking truth to power, working for justice.

There are many sources of inspiration for people dedicated to seeking justice for all the voiceless, human and otherwise. Most inspiring to me are the revolutionary teachings of Jesus, who reflected the love and compassion of God during his life, calling us to radically change the human enterprise, top to bottom.

The called-for change hasn't been implemented very well. The church, inspired by Jesus (not established by him, we need to be reminded), continues to exhibit occasional miraculous enterprises. It also continues with deep flaws. I agree with pastor Robin Meyers that the most important thing about the life of Jesus has been largely lost in many churches of today. Jesus models what we are called to: defiance and resistance to empire and the status quo. I consider myself a 'Christian' follower of Jesus when I feel like overturning tables in sanctuaries of power and writing words that make the Powers That Be and others squirm.

Which brings me to my associate membership in the Iona Community.

The particular issues might be different in Britain, Germany, Malawi or Kenya, but I know that even as I pray for members and associates of the Iona Community each day, I am supported. I don't know how each person bearing these names carries out their particular response to their call from God, but I know they do care about justice, peace and the integrity of creation. I know they do express this through their actions, their worship and through fostering community. So it is a privilege to pray for them, to be blessed with their prayers, and to know that my little contribution to bettering the world is part of a larger whole.

This brings solace and inspiration. When views of people vary so radically, some of us need reminding that we are not crazy or alone.

That I care about my carbon footprint, eat locally and/or choose to buy fair-traded items when I can, that I decry the economic inequality in this country and strive to elect representatives who will try to change that – knowing that there are others within the Iona Community who share these goals is crucial to my sanity at times. Although distances make it hard for our Family Group to meet but once a year, I know their prayers are with me, as mine are with them. This helps my heart and my work, and sooths my despair.

A light breeze scurries across the lake in front of me. The sun warms my face. Changes will come to this lake; it is inevitable. But with wildness, faith, and justice-seeking people, hope endures.

Katharine M Preston

Note:

1.   Rabbi Michael Lerner, from 'God and Goddess Emerging', *Tikkun*, July 22, 2014

At Bethany: Free to be

Yes,
of course I was scandalised, shocked
by my sister's behaviour at the banquet
we held in the Master's honour,
expressing our undying gratitude,
to celebrate our brother's incredible
return from the bonds of death
and the tomb.

At this celebration supper there
was only rejoicing – no time
for teaching, or sitting at the foot
of a respected Rabbi, like lads
receiving their learning
in school.

She had been such a help all day,
in the kitchen, waiting on the men
as they ate – exactly what women
have done in every generation.
She's growing up at last, I thought.
Then this!

She came in meekly enough,
carrying her precious alabaster jar,
left as a dowry by our father.
I have one exactly the same.
I polished it yesterday before
the guests arrived and put it back
on the shelf in the cupboard –
the only place in the house
with a lock.

She knelt on the floor in front of him
and broke the seal – the exotic perfume
pervaded the place, its heavy scent
almost took our breath away.
Her audacious actions did that
when she removed her veil, allowing
her hair to fall freely, hanging loose
and lustrous in front of the entire
company.

Slowly she poured the expensive
ointment over his calloused feet,
washing them first with her tears
and tenderly wiping them, as though
there were only the two of them
in the room, only the two of them
in the world.

It was such an intimate, private
moment, it seemed almost intrusive
to watch; till Judas jealously broke
the silence with his caustic comment
about the poor, voicing the acute
embarrassment
of us all.

The Master, as always, saw past
her generous gesture and looked
into all our hearts, commending her
for what she did, while the rest of us
felt shamed – not by her lavish love,
but by our own meagre
response.

So, yes, I was shocked
and scandalised; of all the people
gathered there that night, only
my little sister, Mary, had the heart
to act upon her impulsive intuition
and serve the Lord, without restraint,
casting aside the bonds of convention,
letting go of dignity and pride,
to give her all.

Carol Dixon

Maundy Thursday

Maundy Thursday footwashing: Peter speaks (1)

It was an embarrassing moment;
piling into the upper room, only
to discover the door servant wasn't there –
he's the one who usually washes feet.
We threw off our cloaks on the cushioned couches
and sat, awkwardly, preferring not to recline –
no one wants to rest his head
next to his neighbour's hot and dusty feet.

We knew that one of us should have got up
and served the others; but on the way here
we'd all grandly put our case for which of us
would be the greatest, would sit
in the highest seat in his coming kingdom;
menial tasks weren't on our menu.

And so he took the basin and the towel,
stripped himself of all but his humanity,
knelt on the floor in front of each one
of us, and gently bathed our feet.
He wasn't even acting out the duties
of a slave; in that moment he became
the lowest of the low.

There was no way I'd let him
touch my feet – abase himself
before me! He was my Master
and my Lord, for God's sake.
I couldn't comprehend why
he should do this when
it should have been me,
their so-called leader,
or one of us at least.

'Never!' I said, recoiling away from him.
I remember his reply to this day.
'If I don't, then you won't belong to me.'
I thought back to the time on the boat,
that very first day when I fell at his feet.
'Then, Lord, wash me all over,' I said.
'Bathe me, in your beauty, and your love.'

Carol Dixon

Maundy Thursday denial: Peter speaks (2)

I told him I'd die for him, you know,
that night in the upper room,
and I meant it. He just looked at me
with that knowing smile of his,
and slightly shook his head, while his eyes
bored into my soul with such love
as he said he knew I wouldn't.
I didn't believe him, of course –
none of us did – we were all so sure
of ourselves, our faith in him,
in the future.

Even later on, standing in the courtyard
by the flickering firelight, when I denied
I knew him, it was like someone else
speaking, it couldn't be me.
Or so I thought, until he looked at me
as they brought him out, battered, bruised,
draped in the purple robe, with that cruel crown
on his bleeding head, like a parody
of a puppet king.

They say Pilate asked him if he was a king.
I wouldn't know. I don't speak Latin or Greek,

but John knew the interpreter –
John has quite a few friends in high places,
which was how we came to be in the courtyard
in the first place, standing by the charcoal fire.
Every time I smell one now, I remember.

I told him I'd die for him,
yet, when it came to it,
I suppose he died for me,
for all of us.
What kind of king does that?

Carol Dixon

Poverty and passion: A reflection for Maundy Thursday

Director of Church Action on Poverty (CAP), Niall Cooper, shares an Easter message. This piece was first published on the CAP website.

Looking at the world this Holy Week, it feels that there is a real need for the new life and rebirth of Easter. And it's not just hoping that the winter and snow will finally end.

Poverty and hunger still have a grip on too many people in the UK, sweeping them to the edges of our society and denying them a say in decisions that affect them. During Lent, we heard, yet again, politicians denying that poverty exists here, or claiming not to understand how unjust policies leave people homeless or hungry.

Those attitudes trap people in poverty and divide communities with stigma and shame, rather than helping to build the just and compassionate society which most of us want to live in.

That is in stark contrast to the Gospel stories we hear today, Maundy Thursday. The Last Supper inspires Christians with a vision of togetherness, sharing food and hospitality. And by washing his disciples' feet, Jesus shows how the kingdom of heaven turns all of our assumptions upside down. The powerful should be servants of the vulnerable, rather than stigmatising, punishing and excluding them.

Those stories will be in our minds at Church Action on Poverty as we continue our work after Easter, and we invite Christians everywhere to join us: *www.church-poverty.org.uk*

Niall Cooper

Why won't he let us sleep?: In the garden of Gethsemane

Why won't he let us sleep? I'm so tired. We've been on the road with him for months and months, hardly ever stopped, different bed every night. We've stood alongside him while he took on the Pharisees, after he healed someone on the Sabbath. We've comforted people in distress, held children up to see him, gone ahead and made sure we all had somewhere to sleep.

Why won't he let us sleep? We're all exhausted. We hardly ever see our families, and it's all very well for him to say we have to care more for him than for our wives and children, for our ageing parents. They have to fend for themselves while we're on the road with him. I worry about my son. He's ten and a bit of a handful for my wife on her own. I love them: it's my duty as a good Jew to care for them and provide for them. I'm exhausted. Why won't he let us sleep?

Why won't he let us sleep? There's obviously trouble coming. He's crossed the Pharisees more than once. Judas left the table early and I'm worried about what he's up to. The powers in Jerusalem don't like Jesus, that's obvious. They've been looking for a way to trap him for some time now. Anything could happen in the next few days – we need all the sleep we can get.

Why won't he let us sleep? He's been under that tree now for hours, praying, talking softly, in a world of his own. I don't know what more we could do to show him we're with him. Then he comes over and asks why we're sleeping.

Couldn't we watch with him, he said. Watch with him? What have we been doing for three hard years? Watched, guarded him, made all the arrangements ahead of him. Sometimes we didn't get much sleep.

To tell you the truth, I would like to sleep till the trouble is over. I stayed awake all night when my baby girl was dying. She could hardly breathe and all my wife and I could do was hold her, keep her warm till she took her last breath. After we had buried her I slept for days. I know what it's like to stay awake while someone is dying. Who would want to do that again?

But we will of course. Whatever tomorrow brings we will be there, standing close to him, whatever happens. But now, in the comforting dark of the garden, I just want to sleep.

Anna Briggs

Good Friday

Road to Calvary

In 2017 associate member of the Iona Community Peter Phillips completed a 40-day pilgrimage to Iona – raising £9100 for Christian Aid's work with refugees, and for the Iona Abbey Capital Appeal …

I vividly remember standing before the Bishop of Lichfield as he sprinkled holy water over me. 'Go in the name of Christ, and may He walk beside you at every step.'

Ahead of me lay 412 miles to Iona Abbey. I had walked Ben, our black lab, every day, but had never tackled anything like this – alone.

Many friends who had come to see me off expressed their concern for my welfare. 'Now, phone me if you get in trouble,' demanded one of the Cathedral vergers. 'I'll drive straight up to you.' That was over two years ago now. 16th March, 2017. Miles and miles of pavement, grass verges, open road, footpaths, towpaths and lanes leading to hamlets, villages, towns and cities, where I was welcomed – night after solitary night.

From Jerusalem to the Sea of Galilee is an eight-day trek, in some of the harshest conditions on earth. Jesus and his followers must have endured unbelievable hardship as they walked from one to the other and back again. But that journey of hardship was but nothing compared to the 'other' journey Jesus was on … the journey to the Cross.

Jesus always knew that his own personal pilgrimage would end on Calvary, in undeniable humiliation … not to mention the gut-wrenching pain, which was not spoken of to his disciples … he kept it to himself.

On my walk from Lichfield Cathedral to Iona Abbey I remember, in certain places, hearing the cry of curlews, cuckoos and seeing foxes and roe deer. These were kindly reminders to me that the Bishop's words were being fulfilled and that Jesus Christ was indeed walking beside me every step of the way … but little did I know then that, within months, I would be on a different journey … a journey where I would need Jesus by my side again.

Two years later I lay on the couch. My Consultant Neurologist lifted up my right leg, then my left. It was obvious to him that I had lost a considerable amount of muscle around the thigh area. I had undergone respiratory tests just a few days before, so now the doctor was fully conversant with my physical condition.

'Get dressed please,' he said quietly. Then: 'I have to tell you that you have motor neurone disease ... I am very, very sorry.'

Was this my pilgrimage to Calvary? Is this what I had lived 67 years to hear? What now lies ahead?

Undeniable humiliation? Not to mention gut-wrenching pain? Obviously, since my diagnosis, I have thought a great deal about it ... often at three o'clock in the morning. Apparently it is a rare condition – only 5,000 sufferers of MND in the UK at any one time, and it bears no connection to my walk to Iona.

MND has a general prognosis of 2 to 4 years. I have truly come up with the notion that my diagnosis of motor neurone disease is a 'gift from God'.

I mentioned this to my Bishop the other day. He took a gulp and said, 'That is harsh, isn't it?' 'Well, yes,' I said. 'But so was crucifixion.'

If we modern-day Christians are to take our faith at all seriously, we must recognise, and be prepared to take, the rough with the smooth ... the harshness with the compassion ... the pain with the joy.

Several friends have commented that I must feel angry. No, I am not angry. I wish I had not been diagnosed with MND, but did Jesus want to go to the Cross?: 'Take this cup from me; yet not my will, but yours be done' (Mt 26:39). He accepted the Cross with humility. This was the will of His Father.

After 12 months ... how am I?

Fine, thanks. My ability to walk any distance at all has now left me, but I am not yet tied to a wheelchair. My voice has altered, due to a weakness of the throat muscles – I can still speak, and plan to read the lesson in the Cathedral next week!

Yes, I have feelings of low mood, just like everyone else.

Yes, Jesus did walk beside me on my pilgrimage to Iona.

But I know, beyond doubt, that He is still beside me … as I walk the road to Calvary.

Peter Phillips

Easter address at Faslane submarine base, April 12, 2014

Good Friday draws nigh, and again we stand outside this nuclear submarine base at Faslane, gathered in this act of public worship, this Witness for Peace of Scottish Christians Against Nuclear Arms.

We stand – including Catholic Archbishop, Church of Scotland Convener, and me a Quaker – drawn from the folds of many different denominations, the underlying undivided Christian Church that prays: 'Thy kingdom come.'

Not Caesar's kingdom come, but God's; and so Pontius Pilate asked Jesus, 'Are you a king, then?' To which the Prince of Peace replied: 'King is your word.' And he spoke unto Pilate of non-violence, saying: 'My kingdom is not of this world. If it was, my followers would fight' (John 18:36–37).

Likewise, when the disciple cut off the ear of the high priest's servant, Jesus disarmed him, saying: 'Put away your sword, Peter … No more of this!' (John 18:11, Luke 22:51). Why? Because violence destroys our ability to hear one another. Christ healed the ear and healed our hearing, therefore Easter asks us: can we hear the deeper whisperings of the Cross? The Cross of wood and nails encircled with a crown of thorns that stood upon a green hill far away. The Cross of monstrous hulls and thermonuclear warheads surrounded by a barbed wire fence that is this Trident missile base today.

The Bible claims that Christ came 'to give his life, as a ransom' (Mark 10:45, Matthew 20:28, 1 Timothy 2:6), and so, to a central question of the Cross: Who – is the ransomer of souls?

Throughout the first millennium the church's main answer was the Devil. Christ 'descended into Hell' and his suffering was the ransom price that purchased our whole salvation.

Early in the second millennium, Anslem, the Archbishop of Canterbury, argued that this gave the Devil too much power. Who, then, could be the ransomer of souls? Only one other candidate in town was qualified to take the post.

Christ's death, Anslem reasoned, 'satisfied' a God whose feudal honour human sin had offended. Later, John Calvin sharpened this up into the penal substitution theory of the Atonement. God was 'armed for vengeance', but out of love for the Elect, and they alone, sent Christ to take their punishment.

The problem with such blood atonement is its seeming sanction of redemptive violence. A God armed for vengeance nods too readily towards the blasphemous idolatry of *HMS Vengeance* here at Faslane; and that, beneath a sovereign Commander in Chief, who doubles as Defender of the Faith.

What then, for this third millennium, might be the meaning of the Cross? Who, or what, this ransomer of souls? Whither a liberation theory of 'atonement'?

I came today from Govan further up the Clyde; many of my neighbours ransomed unto violence through its face of poverty. That draws me to a single paragraph in a book, *Mon Dieu, Pourquoi?*, where the late Abbé Pierre, a radical French priest, wrote of his wrestling with the ransom question. Was it the Devil, or God? he'd asked. Then came his breakthrough: 'The drug addict,' he wrote, '... *is at the same time his own executioner and the victim. He is both the ransomer and the hostage ... It is the same with all human beings. Because we are disconnected from our authentic divine source, we have become our own executioners. We are slaves to our disordered desires, to our egotism.*'[1]

The Cross, the supreme transformative symbol of non-violence, absorbs in its forgiveness all chains that bind us. Here is the love that dies for love, yet being of eternity, never dies. And so, 'we call this Friday good'.

Christ said: 'I come to bring fire to the earth, and wish it were already kindled!' (Luke 12:49). Let us listen with our healing ear. What kind of fire?

The fire of Hell, of Trident's holocaust? Or the fire of love. That is why we witness at Faslane. That is why we bite the bullet, so unfashionably; why we today survey the wondrous Cross.

Alastair McIntosh

Note:

1.   From *Mon Dieu, Pourquoi?*, Abbé Pierre, Plon, Paris, 2005, pp. 69–70, translated by Alastair McIntosh

Why?

From the Defence of Brian Quail (a member of the Iona Community), on trial at Dumbarton JP Court on 12 October, 2017 for the blockade of Coulport on 11 July 2017. RNAD Coulport is the storage and loading facility for the nuclear warheads of the UK's Trident missile programme.

… Let me finish on a personal note.

Several years ago I had heart surgery – a double bypass. This was at the time when Trident warheads were first being sent up to Scotland from Burghfield in Berkshire.

The good folk of Faslane Peace Camp, John Ainslie, the administrator of SCND, and myself regularly used to follow these convoys and hold them up whenever we could safely do so.

I had noticed that every time I saw the convoy, and heard the particular sickening roar of the Foden carriers, I would get intense chest pains. This got worse and worse, until finally things came to a head on one occasion when we stopped the convoy at Whistlefield roundabout, up from the

North Gate of Faslane. The lead vehicle was stopped and I ran up to support the action. The pains grew more and more intense. I collapsed on the road in agony. People crowded round and someone said, 'We'll need to take him to the hospital.' I said, 'No, I'll be OK. Leave me here.'

The pains were unbearable, like tiger's claws in my chest. I thought: *This is it. I am dying.* Then I thought: *Why am I dying here, on the road beside a vehicle carrying nuclear bombs?*

I looked up at a patch of blue in the sky, and it reminded me of my youngest daughter Catherine, who has particularly lovely blue eyes. Then I thought, *No, it's not just my children's blue eyes, but the green eyes, and the brown eyes, and the grey eyes of all the children – and their mothers and fathers too – who are the target of our bombs. Our fellow human beings, our brothers and sisters, whom we are prepared to burn, blast and irradiate.*

And I knew the answer to my question Why? It is love that drives me. Love is not an emotional or sentimental feeling. As Dostoyevsky said, *'active love is a harsh and fearful thing' (The Brothers Karamazov).* It is not what you say, it is what you do.

So I am not to be stereotyped as a peace protestor, I am – though I don't look it – a lover …

Brian Quail

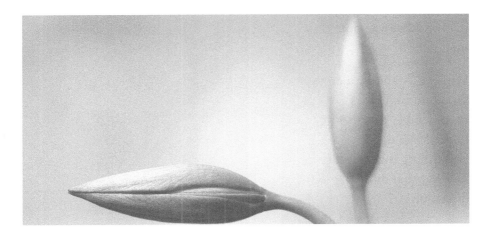

Who will stand by a cross?

Written in response to the commemorations of the 100th anniversary of the First World War.

Who will stand by a cross
for a hundred years,
to remember the child
who died by chance,
from a random shot
in a war that was not
for freedom?

Who will stand by a cross
for a hundred years,
to remember the girl
abused by troops,
spoil of the win,
in a war that was not
last resort?

Who will stand by a cross
for a hundred years,
to remember the home
that huddled in fear
as the drone lurked by,
in a war that was not
understood?

Who will stand by a cross
for a hundred years,
to remember the ones
hunted like dogs
for tending the wounds,
in a war that did not
discriminate?

Who will stand by a cross
for a hundred years,
to remember the ones
who took up the gun
and killed and died
in a war that was not
the end?

Tim Aldred

Mates to die for

'Mates at the "Mallet and Nails"'
they joked, and shrugged.
'Drinkers at Death's cup;
leaves left hanging on a dead tree.'
Then hoisted us, a pitiless exhibit,
to writhe together,
hanging between earth and air,
comrades on the gibbet of the sky.
You might not choose
to share such anguish with a stranger
but I would have chosen these,
and slung between them
shared the hours it took to die.

Friends who had walked with me fled
and left me naked.
But these two, tied and skewered
with me, shared their bleak humanity.
One cursed his fate
and mocked my helplessness.
I heard him, raging at a God
who stood aloof from all the grievance of his life,
not knowing that I bled

alongside always. Eternity
will quieten all his raving disbelief.

The other turned
and gave me all he had, his pain
and broken hopes,
called me by name and fixed his eyes of agony
on mine.
He shared the hours of darkness with me,
reminded me of why I came
as thirst and pain consumed all thought
and prayer deserted me. He
befriended me, despite
the ultimate aloneness of our dying.

I waited for him. Led him laughing
into light, into the green
garden, by the quiet paths,
the sweet water,
beneath the shade of trees
of never-failing leaf.

Janet Killeen

Three Good Friday prayers for those living with memory loss

In these prayers, we hold all those who are living with memory loss or confusion, those living with a diagnosis of dementia, and all those who love
and care for them.

Forgive your forgets (Luke 23:34)

I only met Simon recently. When he speaks his eyes are alight with joy,
revealing the radiance of his soul – there is no hiding Simon's light under
any bushel!

Simon told me that he had been frustrated by his failing memory for a while, often feeling impatient and at times berating himself for his lapses. So he felt relief when he was given a diagnosis, an explanation, and a sign-post for his journey.

'In the car on the way home from hospital,' Simon explained, 'I thought: Well, if this is my dying then I shall follow the way of Jesus!' And he resolved to use Christ's prayers from the cross as his guide.

He went on to say, 'I was meditating on the first of Jesus' prayers on the cross, "Father, forgive them, for they know not what they do." I puzzled for a moment, and then I actually experienced "a light" and the words you must "forgive your forgets". I was uplifted!'

Simon's acceptance and courage in facing his journey is testimony to his deep faith. Simon has generously shared his thoughts with me in this prayer:

Lord, who must I forgive? No one has wronged me.
I do not suffer at the hands of others as you did,
as so many people of our world do.
I am one of the fortunate ones.

My love is not thrown back at me,
my life not taken from me.
My words are not twisted,
my voice is not silenced,
my hands are not tied,
my body is not tortured.

Lord, who must I forgive?

And you whispered into my soul:
'You must forgive your forgets.
For the times you want to help, but cannot find the words;
for the times you try to do the right thing, but get in a muddle;
for the times a name won't come to you,
or you are puzzled by what you are doing,

and you torture yourself;
it is yourself you must forgive.'

'Forgive your forgets,' you said,
'for as I forgive you, so you should forgive,
even yourself.'

Don't forsake me (Mark 15:34)

I met Joan when she came to stay at the hospice where I worked. An aggressive brain tumour left her feeling disorientated and struggling with her memory. Joan's faith had been a deep comfort to her throughout her life, but she found herself despairing that she felt she could no longer pray now that she couldn't remember who she was praying to. Joan's experience inspired this prayer:

Lord, how did I get so lost?
When did I lose you?
I know that I knew you,
but where are you now
when I need you most?

I am terrified.
I feel myself falling into darkness
with no light, no end;
there is no one to catch me,
nothing to hold on to!

And how can I pray
when I can't remember who you are,
or your words of promise to me?

Hold me firmly, Lord,
and when I fall keep me safe,
for you know how it feels when you're lost.

Into your hands (Luke 23:46)

Sheila's dementia is very advanced. She lives in a nursing home, where she often sits quietly, nursing a toy doll. When Sheila's family visit, sometimes she appears to recognise them, but usually she does not. A woman who is a wife, mother and grandmother, who has a wisdom and compassion borne out of a long, often tough, life, she is now withdrawn and distanced from those whom she loves most. She appears to feel safe and comfortable, and this brings comfort to those who love her. And, although Sheila cannot chew her food, a creamy cake always goes down extremely well!

Lord, now I surrender myself,
and rest in the care and prayers of others.
Let me feel you in the gentle touch of a hand on my skin;
know your warmth in the glow of the sun on my face.
May I recognise you in the sweet flavour and rich pleasure of cake;
your familiar voice in the tune of a song;
the stirrings of love in the searching gaze of a 'stranger'.

Meet me in the early-morning light,
and the evening's gentle sigh;
and when it is time for me to leave,
for the veil to part and the Sun to break through,
greet me in your Rising Place,
the land that has always been home.

Elaine Gisbourne

This poem changes nothing

A poem inspired by 2019 Iona Community Continentals Week in the Nether-lands, the theme of which was 'the joy of creation'.

The house is burning down: It's time to act.

Words laden with meaning.
The wonder of the moon, the stars, the sun.
The beauty of the babbling brook.
The scudding of the clouds.
Gathering on a sun-kissed morning.
Vibrant grasses, scent of flowers,
lichen on the rocks, tang of seaweed.
Words convey beauty.
The joy of creation.

But the house is burning down: It's time to act.

How many words will it take to save the planet?
How many studies, symposia?
How many researchers, reports, resolutions?
How many texts, treatises, tomes, theological talks?
Millions, billions of words.

But the house is burning down: It's time to act.

No amount of words can stop the spread of Saharan sand.
No stanza has ever stopped a single ton of CO_2 being spat forth
from a coal-fired power station.
No sonnet has halted the inexorable rise of the sea.
No song has saved a single species from extinction.
Words have power, so they say.

But the house is burning down: It's time to act.

The house is burning down.
It is real and it is happening.

Already one degree hotter.
Already halfway to the tipping point
at which global warming will become irreversible.
Already sea levels are rising at the fastest level for three thousand years.
Already a sixty per cent drop in wildlife populations.
Already as much CO_2 as three million years ago,
when sea levels were metres higher and trees grew at the South Pole.

The house is burning down: It's time to act.

The younger generation say:
'Unite behind the science,
unite behind the science,
that is our demand.
We must hold the older generations accountable
for the mess they have created ...
We cannot solve a crisis without treating it as a crisis ...
if solutions within the system are so impossible to find,
then ... we should change the system itself.'

The house is burning down: It's time to act.

Act as if the planet depended on it.
Act as if it mattered.
Act as if it, the house, was burning down,
because the house is burning down.
Act as if it was a climate emergency.
Act to challenge the status quo.
Act to challenge the notion that nothing
and no one needs to really change:
as long as I drive a little less, fly a little less,
use a little less plastic, eat a little less meat,
smile a bit more, recycle a bit more, do my little bit,
the world will be a better place.
And 'all things will be well, and all manner of things will be well'.
All manner of things will not be well.

The house is burning down: It's time to act.

Act with others.
Act with courage.
Act out of our comfort zones, out of love for our planet.
Act out of outrage at the lack of action.
Act to disrupt the status quo.
Act to disinvest from the fossil-fuel-fuelled financers
and fossil-fuelled fabricators of fictions
that fracking is fine and fossil fuel is fine, as long as it's our fossil fuel.
Act to keep it in the ground.
Act to close the roads.
Act to close the coal-fired power stations.
Act to stop more runways.
Act to stop the fracking.
Act to open minds.
Act to open minds to the possibility
that action changes anything, everything.
Act to show 'that a small group of thoughtful, committed citizens can
change the world:
it's the only thing that ever has'.[1]

The house is burning down: It's time to act.

Words change nothing.
This poem will change nothing.
Unless we act.
Decisively.
And now.

The house is burning down: It's time to act.

Niall Cooper

Note:

1. Margaret Mead

Holy Saturday

Waiting

Serena and I have been best friends for longer than we haven't. We met aged 11 in high school, and 12 years later we still seek wisdom and laughter from each other.

A few years ago Serena became very ill with the eating disorder anorexia nervosa. She was forced to leave her studies at university to find shelter, healing and peace at home. We all hoped that she would find space to improve her physical and mental condition once she was in close proximity to her family and childhood home.

It wasn't long before it became apparent that it was impossible to plan a nice and simple recovery. Serena deteriorated, which created a hidden but steadily growing sense of panic and frustration in all who loved her. Serena spent thousands of hours talking to therapists, doctors and dieticians. Nothing seemed to help.

Perhaps inevitably, it became necessary to send Serena to a recovery centre, 145 miles away from home, where she would become an inpatient for an indistinguishable amount of time. There Serena would be cared for 24 hours a day by a pick-and-mix selection of medical professionals, social advisors, therapists, nutritionists, dieticians and trained supervisors. Serena would be placed on a necessarily strict daily regime, with no one but paid strangers to comfort her. As terrifying as the prospect seemed to us, her friends and family, Serena must have felt that dread three-fold. She was finally being forced to face herself, go into a place where all her ultimate fears would be tackled every single day without rest. She was forced to enter the recovery centre with no idea of when she might be discharged, little idea of the realities of what she would face and minimal contact with the outside world.

No one doubted that this was necessary, but the feeling of helpless devastation that this was the reality of Serena's situation was all too powerful. It was like that feeling when you walk up the stairs in the dark, and mistakenly think that there is one more step at the top, only to feel that sickening feeling when your foot falls too far. I felt like I had missed a step in life when Serena was sent away. Just for that moment I was falling, without knowing when the ground would rise up and steady me once again. I will never forget that physical and emotional sensation of watching my best friend being sent away to an unknown place of suffering and fear, and knowing that this was an essential course of action.

The helpless love I felt during that time was unbearable. I would not wish that upon anyone, and yet I know that most people have experienced this feeling in some way. No words can aptly describe the total mix of stomach-twisting, heart-wrenching, fist-clenching emotion I felt when watching my dearest friend manoeuvre through the darkest parts of her life. During this time I felt suspended between grief and hopeful anticipation. Waiting to hear news from anyone. Trying to navigate my own life with Serena still extremely present in everything I did. I was told that Serena's time at the recovery centre would come to an end at some point, but as months began to pass, her discharge seemed no closer. Our waiting refused to end.

On Good Friday, Jesus was put to death in front of all his closest friends. Here, I view Jesus as a man, a son and a friend, not simply as the son of God. Having watched my best friend go through so much pain alone, I may have a small insight into how the disciples might have felt on that day. They watched their beloved friend sent away to a unknown fearful place to experience unimaginable suffering. When Serena was sent away I felt guilt that I had failed her in some way. I cannot doubt that each one of Jesus' disciples felt something similar. At his death, Jesus was within touching distance, and yet, the disciples could do nothing. Disbelief, too, must have plagued the mind of each friend who watched Jesus' death. Just as I asked: how is this happening to my best friend? It cannot be happening because this isn't how I wanted things to happen. This isn't how I imagined things to happen.

It was impossible to tell, in Serena's case, if what we had stretching out before us was indeed a wait, or if it was simply the new reality. Was Serena even going to be discharged, or would she turn into one of those terrible stories where recovery is truly not going to be possible? For Jesus' best friends, those three days must have felt impossible to navigate. Those three days belong to the disciples in a way that none of us can claim: we know that Jesus returned, Jesus' disciples did not. Not everything that belongs to us is easy to own, and yet, that doesn't make it any less precious. I would never wish a wait like I experienced upon anyone, but I would not want it removed from my past. During that time I truly learnt what it was to be a friend. I stubbornly tried my best to help Serena see that she wasn't alone in her suffering, although I don't doubt she felt alone more often than she didn't. The odd letter, gift and visit was all I could do. And for the invisible tie of friendship that was more than enough. Jesus' disciples did all they could: perfuming his body, placing it in a tomb and meeting illegally together. They stuck steadfastly together, and that was how Jesus found them, three days after his death.

Waiting is hell. During the wait we may feel that we contribute nothing and nothing we do makes any difference at all. But I was surprised, in hindsight, at how much I did contribute while I felt that way, and only by speaking to Serena have I learnt what a difference it made. The disciples did what they could and, regardless of how they must have felt, it was exactly what they needed to do. I learnt that, for me, helplessness is a feeling and not a fact. I learnt that waiting is anything but easy, and yet it can be so valuable.

Laura Gisbourne

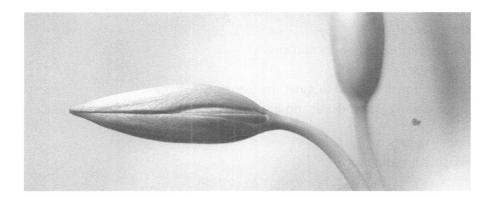

Easter

Only then can we sing Alleluia

No
Alleluia
is
sung in Lent.

Instead, we proclaim:
'Return even now,' says the Lord,
'return to me with all your heart, with fasting,
and with mourning; and rend your hearts
and not your garments.

Return to the Lord, your God, for he is
gracious and merciful,
slow to anger,
and abounding in steadfast love.' (Joel 2:12–13)

We are not convinced.

On Thursday
we sing no Alleluias.
Instead we beg, bargain, confess, cajole, lament,
tremble in fear, hope beyond hope,
get down on our knees,
crawl to the table –
share a meal,
and memories and hopes and angers,
even a few laughs
to cover the dread and to quiet the cavern of fear
in the ocean of dark death and loss.

Friday comes.
We sing no Alleluias.

How can the world suffer such cruelty and loss?
Tacked to a tree!
Man's cruelty knows no bounds!
We are swallowed by chaos, confusion, loss.
Not willing to face the loss and grief we walk
seven miles to Nokesville or Smithwich or
Emmaus – any no-where –
just somewhere away from the loss.
We sing no Alleluias tonight
because we have seen with our own eyes that all is lost.
Everything.
Our ears are shut to hopeful invitations.

Saturday –
we sing no Alleluias on this day either.
What is there to do this day
but to fill time, in the meantime?
To escape the great 'NO' of Friday.
Saturday
is in the meantime,
to be filled with shopping, sweeping, fixing leaks, having sex,
viewing action movies to cover our boredom, drinking.
Getting through the day
to cover flat emptiness of time without meaning.
Saturday is the showstopper all right!
But not in a good way.
It's the day when it dawns on us that we have no hope;
no hope for undoing what has happened.
Saturday can last a lifeless lifetime.
A choice must be made.
It *is*
the day to face and move
from
grief to mourning –
the only way to the YES of Sunday!

It is the only way to get to the morning sunrise –
we can mourn what we have lost –
to face the fact of life's aches and limitations,
and heave loud sobs –
the only language our hearts now speak.

Only those who fully enter this dark and uncertain terrain called NO …
only they find their way home again to the YES of Sunday.
To their God – who is
gracious and
merciful and
abounding in steadfast love.

Only then,
can we sing
Alleluia
on Easter Morn!

Benjamin Pratt

Easter Morning: Mary

He spoke my name.
That was how I knew it was him.
No one ever said my name
like that, before, or since.
I'd had to get out of the city –
the claustrophobic confines
of the upper room, the sombre
atmosphere, forced conversation,
drove me mad; so I stumbled
down the outside stair onto
the quiet paving stones below
and followed my feet.

I wasn't aware of where I was heading
but found myself back in the garden.
I hadn't meant to go there
yet when I reached the place I thought
at least I'd be doing something;
replacing the spices, rearranging
the grave clothes, anything
to keep me close to him.

Then I remembered the stone,
the huge boulder blocking the way,
sealed with Caesar's insignia,
ringed round with Roman guards.
I couldn't bear to turn back,
empty-hearted, now I'd come so close,
so I pressed on, hoping against hope
for a miracle, just a small something –
a kindly soldier, or friendly passer-by –
so I could see him just once more,
at peace.

Not like the last time:
barely cold, broken, lying
in his anguished mother's arms
as we struggled to do the right thing
and prepare his battered body
before the Sabbath curfew began.

But when I reached the tomb – nothing!
No seal, no stone, no body;
an empty shell with no one inside.
O God! Don't say they've taken him,
defiled in death the body of the Man
I loved; who loved me, and all who
followed, with the passionate love of God.

I looked around frantically and,
in the distance, I espied a figure
in the burgeoning daylight, silhouetted
by the brightening rays of early sun.
Thank God! The gardener.
I hastened to him, falling at his feet:
'Oh, sir,' I said, 'if you know
who has taken him, tell me,
so I can go and get him.'

And then I heard my name,
spoken, as if I'd never heard it before:
'Mary!' and I knew. In that moment
I knew everything.
He gently prised my grasping hands
aside and raised me to my feet,
and bade me tell the others
he would see them, back in Galilee.
He spoke my name.
And all my world was filled with joy –
the joy of a new beginning.

Carol Dixon

Salted with fire

I have a feeling that we might look back at this time, the half century from around 1970 to 2020, as having been the zenith of secular materialism. A time when the vacuity of the human condition collapsed into an urgent and emergent thirst to recover mystery from out of barren egocentric reasoning. To recover spiritual imagination.

The problem with ungrounded intellect is that reality is incomplete when it is not rested in the heart. The Hindus have a central mantra. *Om mani padme hum.* It means that the *Om,* the cosmic totality of being, is realised when the *mani,* the diamond of the mind, rests in the *padme,* the lotus of the heart, *hum,* undivided.

Jesus says the same in Luke 17. The community of heaven will not be found in the logical ordering of the rational world. It's not something that you find in the realm of 'Here it is!' or 'There it is!' The community of heaven is within. Then we will be enlightened, Luke goes on to say, and so poetically in the King James Version, 'as the lightning, that lighteneth out of the one part under heaven, shineth unto the other part under heaven'. Then we will see the inner truth of all.

A lightning show is best watched in the darkness. Our eyes must similarly grow accustomed to the spiritual milieu. We will not see with eyes that have been dazzled and damaged by too much outer world reality. The saints would turn off artificial lights; they'd fast as Easter drew nigh. Theology itself, when seen through damaged eyes, turns toxic. It turns us from within back to the busy, noisy realm of 'here' or 'there'. We miss the rhythms of the mystery, their many layers of meaning, we maybe even cast them out – anathema! – and lose them to our shared traditions.

Consider hell. Those who take a literal fundamentalist view of Christian scripture often point to the binary divide between Heaven and Hell posited in the story of Lazarus and Dives. But dim the lights a little, watch for the underflash of lightning from the clouds, and the word used in Luke 16 is simply Hades, the Greek world of the afterlife. Moreover, in addressing Dives – the corporate banker, the arms merchant, the human trafficker, the ordinary me and you – Abraham refers to him tenderly, as 'son' or 'child'. It's not exactly unredemptive language.

Or consider Matthew 3, where Christ comes with his winnowing fork to separate the wheat from the chaff, and to burn the latter in unquenchable fire. This is another passage that's used to justify a binary divide between heaven and hell, the Elect and the Damned. But not so fast. Have too many theologians up their ivory towers been set loose on this passage? Is it not the case that every single grain of wheat has had its corresponding chaff? That, as vital to its growing journey? Might we not be wiser, and more humble towards others, if we take our cue from 1 Corinthians 3, and understand it as the fire that tests the quality of each one of us, the fire that refines gold?

Then there's Mark's Gospel, chapter 9, where Jesus seems to open all the stops on hell, for here, repeated three times, 'their worm dieth not, and the fire is not quenched'. Note, however, that the rhetorical force of this text has been amplified through time. Modern translations tend to omit verses 44 and 46, leaving only verse 48, as the repetitions are lacking in the most reliable early manuscripts.

Still, 'the fire that never shall be quenched' sounds bad enough. But if we read on, if we don't quote out of context, the remaining verses in the chapter say: 'For everyone shall be salted with fire … Salt is good … Have salt in yourselves, and have peace one with another.' Salt was a precious commodity and it brings out the flavour, so here too is a metaphor of our winnowing.

The first letter of John, chapter 4, tells that perfect love casts out fear because fear is punishment, or torment. Because 'God is love.'

Easter exposes naked violence on a green hill far away, but devoid of reciprocal violence in a never-ending spiral. Instead, the buck stops here. The cross absorbs the violence of the world. Christ told Pilate that if he was a worldly king, his followers would take up the sword and rally to save him (John 18). His 'kingdom' is not of this world, the very concept of being a 'king', he shows Pilate, is suspect. His way is not of this world. As our medieval forebears might have translated it, 'Thy community of the realm come … in earth as is in heaven.'

Over the Easter weekend, says the Apostles' Creed, 'He descended into Hell.' But as Livvy or John Livingstone, a street theologian and eco-warrior of the GalGael Trust in George MacLeod's Govan once said, 'Hell could not hold such love as this.'

As the Russian Orthodox theologian Paul Evdokimov develops the point: *'The only message which could reach atheism today is that of Christ descending into hell. As deep as the hell in which we find ourselves, it is even more profound to find Christ already there waiting for us.'* [1]

'The fire of hell,' says another Orthodox theologian, Olivier Clément, is but *'the fire of love that gives remorse a terrible clarity.'* [2] It burns off only the chaff, only that which is no longer authentic to us. Such love as this can not be trapped in space and time. It can not be limited to our logical perceptions and cognitions of 'here' or 'there'. Such love is of the mystery, grounded in eternity. Resurrection is intrinsic to the nature of that which never dies, *'You can't kill the Spirit …'* How we tell that story, how we relax the *mani* into the *padme*, how we ground what is in heaven here on earth, well, that is the Easter story.

'Our God is a consuming fire' (Hebrews 12:29).

And there's the lightning flash.

Alastair McIntosh

Notes:

1. Paul Evdokimov, *In the World, of the Church: A Paul Evdokimov Reader*, St Vladimir's Seminary Press, NY, 2001, p.191.

2. Olivier Clément, *The Roots of Christian Mysticism: Texts from the Patristic Era with Commentary*, Olivier Clément, New City Press, NY, 1993, p.303.

Healed within

During Easter Week I was thinking particularly about the ways in which my often faltering Christian faith has supported me since I was diagnosed with an incurable cancer in January 2016. Those of you who have experienced cancer are well aware that some days can be tough-going. Other days are much easier to cope with – and I believe a lot depends on our mental approach to our illness. By that I mean not just depending on drugs – efficient as they may be – but also being aware, day by day, of our mind, our soul and our heart. And of our relationship to the One who holds us all, whether in sickness or in health.

With a long-term, incurable illness it is not difficult to become depressed at times. As patients, we get weary of having to take medicine all the time; we get fed up with our various aches and pains; we wonder what the future holds as we gradually get weaker in our bodies. Even if we are surrounded by loving support of one kind or another, cancer can be a lonely journey. It *is* a lonely journey – which is not to say it does not also contain blessings! It does. Many surprising blessings are held for us within the cancer pathway. And as we know, if you have cancer, there are so many wonderfully supportive networks – not least the Maggie's Centres scattered around Scotland. I have also found encouragement when I read the life stories of others.

Recently I read about the British soldier who had been badly wounded in Afghanistan some years back. His multiple injuries almost destroyed him physically and mentally and he went through long periods of depression. He felt his life was over. Then came the blessing! He took up drawing and painting, and is now regarded as a fine portrait painter with many commissions. In the last few years several awards have come his way. It is a wonderful story. His new-found gift has given him new life and a sense of purpose.

And this brings me to reflect on the inner meaning of Christian healing. Every week, during the last 70 years since the formation of the modern Iona Community, there has been a Service of Healing held within the ancient beauty of Iona Abbey. Over the years hundreds of thousands of people from every corner of the world have taken part in this deeply moving service. Each week in the service we say together the great Iona prayer for healing:

Spirit of the living God,
present with us now,
enter you,
body, mind and spirit,
and heal you of all that harms you,
in Jesus' name.
Amen

I love these words and now, with cancer in my body, they have a new meaning for my life. I know I am not going to be 'cured' and that it is highly likely that at some point I will die from the multiple myeloma which is in my system. Yet I also know that the living God can be with me, day by day, in body, mind and spirit. At the level of mystery and of prayer I do not walk alone. Nor do you. I know from the experiences of my pastoral ministry that we can be very sick in terms of the body yet actually 'healed' within. That may be a paradox to some people but it is true. The spirit, the heart, the mind and the soul can all be in good health, even with a serious illness. I do believe that I need not be diminished spiritually just because I have cancer. Christ's healing reaches out to make us whole in a great number of ways. If I carry bitterness and self-pity and anger in my heart and am full of good health am I really healed? These things can harm us as much as a physical illness. The prayer from Iona reminds us to invite the Holy Spirit into our lives so that *all* that actually harms us can be healed. In that sense we all need deep inner healing. This is the healing of God which comes to all those who seek it. That wonderful truth is at the heart of our Christian faith. Anna Briggs captured that perfectly in one of her beautiful hymns: '*We bring our broken selves, confused and closed and tired; then through your gift of healing grace new purpose is inspired.*'[1]

Peter Millar

Note:

1. Anna Briggs, from 'We lay our broken world'

What is Easter?

'What is Easter?' they ask.
It belongs to the life and love;
it follows the healing and welcome;
it echoes the upturning of tables
and the peacemaking.
It summarises the blessing
on the mount and the breaking
of bread.

Love becomes the cross and its agony;
three days later an empty tomb;
broken bread and fish on the shore;
the mystery of the resurrection
and the turning from despair
to the joy of new beginnings;
new beginnings that we share today.

'What is Easter?' they ask.
It's about the collapse of a wall,
the building of a clinic.
It leads the way to the child
who now walks, the old woman
who can see again,
the bomb that didn't fall,
the clasp of hands, black and brown.
It spells the hope in our hearts,
the glory of reds and yellows in spring,

a gift exploding into a new day,
a gong sounding over and over in ecstasy,
the past crashing into the present,
the present opening doors to eternity.

Judy Dinnen

In the breaking of the bread

We brought a group of Taiwanese and African pastors to the mountains of North Carolina to live in community with a group of American pastors for ten days. One of the Taiwanese pastors was missing his wife and two young children. One morning as he walked by himself to our meeting place, an African-American man got out of his car and greeted him warmly. The man asked the Taiwanese pastor where he was from. The Taiwanese pastor told him that he'd come from Asia to join a week of spiritual community with pastors from all over the world. The man, who happened to be the basketball coach at the college where we were meeting, sensed that the pastor's heart was anxious and invited him to come to his office in the gym next door.

They talked for a while. And then three of the basketball players appeared in his office. The coach asked the pastor, 'Can we pray for you?' The pastor's eyes lit up and he said, 'That would be wonderful.' So the new friends gathered around this Taiwanese pastor and prayed for him and for his family a world away. And then the pastor asked if he could pray for the coach and his players, and they also said, 'That would be wonderful.' They then gave him a jersey from their basketball team, which he wears with joy.

Two disciples were walking along the road, dejected. The one they loved, they thought was far away. But suddenly he joins them on the road. At first they do not recognise him. But then in the breaking of the bread, their eyes are opened and they know that Christ is with them.

On the roads of the mountains in North Carolina, on the streets of Glasgow, on the roads in the teeming city of Taipei, Christ comes and walks with us and listens and shares life.

At that moment, open-eyed, wide-eyed, they recognised him. And then he disappeared. Back and forth they talked. 'They said to each other, "Were not our hearts burning within us while he was talking to us on the road, while he was opening the scriptures to us?"' (Lk 24:32, NRSV).

Easter season is a time for open eyes and open ears. It is a time to pay attention to the One who travels with us.

John McCall, Taipei, Taiwan

Hanging out with friends

'I do not call you servants any longer, because the servant does not know what
the master is doing; but I have called you friends, because I have made known
to you everything that I have heard from my Father.'

John 15:15, NRSV (Easter reading in the Revised Common Lectionary)

For much of my adult life, in response to the question, 'What gets you out
of bed in the morning?' I would have replied: 'the pursuit of justice and
the belief that God takes sides with the poor'. Now, if I am honest, I am
not so sure. Don't get me wrong: these things still matter but the lens feels
like it has shifted. Unjust systems make my blood boil, but it is seeing the
effect that they have on the people I love that forces me to action.

At present, I have friends fighting the inherently unjust immigration system
in the UK. Their right to remain in Scotland – a country they have come
to know and love – has been consistently refused and they face the threat

of being returned to a country in which they fear for their lives. That's why I write to the Home Secretary, go on protest marches and pen statements on behalf of the Church of Scotland.

Through my involvement with the Poverty Truth Commission, I have several friends who have been sanctioned by the Department of Work and Pensions and have, as a result, run out of money and spiralled into poor mental health. It is these friendships which motivate me to try to understand the impenetrable complexity of our benefits system and to call out the deep injustices within it. It is also that friendship which convinces me that we will never have a just social security system until we involve folk like my friends in its design, delivery and ongoing improvement.

Recently, I had the privilege of spending a week at Camas, the Iona Community's outdoor centre on Mull, at Youth Festival with a spectacular group of young men and women, including some utterly outstanding young leaders. Amid all the laughter and banter, as well as while using muscles that have lain dormant for a long time, I was reminded (again) of just how inspiring so many young people are. I want to join them in their passionate hopes for a better world rather than simply imbue them with a burdensome concern for the institutions and organisations I hold dear.

In recent years, I have thought from time to time about Jesus' plea to his disciples that they (we) are to operate more out of a relationship based on friendship as opposed to servanthood (Jn 15:15). Perhaps it's an age thing but I have become tired of serving the poor and railing against injustice particularly in an age when the forces of evil seem very real and progress hard to see. However, I have not become tired of friendships; they matter more than ever. And the privilege – it is actually a deliberate choice – of having so many wonderful and inspiring friends for whom life is a deep struggle continues to motivate, encourage and help me to see sparks of God constantly breaking.

Martin Johnstone

Hearts that beat the same

… I was a stranger and you welcomed me …

Matthew 25:35, NRSV (an Easter reading in various lectionaries)

Living out your commitments to being a member of the Iona Community becomes a lifestyle that evolves wherever you find yourself.

I live in what is described as 'an area of multiple deprivation' in a housing scheme in the east end of Glasgow: not exactly the best place to house asylum seekers and refugees, many of whom were already living in austere and challenging environments.

I, too, am challenged, with being a disabled wheelchair user, living on a basic benefit income, alongside folk struggling to survive.

Living the Gospel and offering hospitality in this environment is very basic, and in my case just started with a smile. As I wheeled through the park on my way to church, noticing there were folk of different nationalities and cultures gathered round, I simply smiled, and acknowledged their existence. Sometimes this developed into saying 'Hi'.

Over time I noticed many of these strangers looked sad and anxious, had inappropriate clothing for the weather, and it materialised they were asylum seekers who had been dispatched to the area, and didn't know anyone or where to go for things.

The other church had a community project, so it would have been easy just to pass folk on to them, but I too had come to the area knowing no one and, as a disabled person, had experienced how difficult it was to get involved in the community. So I felt a degree of responsibility to try to make folk feel welcome.

Over time I noticed a mum and her 10-year-old very hyperactive daughter, who hailed from Pakistan. Mum confided that they were struggling through the asylum process, both having health problems, and needed help to gather support for their case. Having no clue as to what this would entail, I offered to accompany them to all the various venues to get legal advice, medical support, educational guidance, and to the Home Office. I could offer lifts, listen and learn; and in return they invited me to their flat, where I was initiated into Asian food. And as we shared, I was humbled and privileged to hear something of their story, and the horror at what I was hearing made me weep. Mum declared that no one had ever wept with her, and this created a bond that spread over several years as they finally secured their 'leave to remain', by the skin of their teeth; meanwhile I encouraged mum to get her daughter assessed and placed in more appropriate education, again chumming them along to all the necessary appointments.

The intense nature of this involvement had not gone unnoticed, and another mum and daughter, from Africa, requested my support, and I became involved again in helping the daughter get more socially integrated, and in supporting her throughout her mum's three-month hospitalisation.

This led to me being introduced to another African mum and daughter, who subsequently fell foul of the asylum system. And my previous experience led to being able to help them fight their case – resulting in mass community support, where local folk came to realise these strangers were just people like themselves – trying to secure a safe home and build a life and future for their family.

This family did get removed to a detention centre; and I found myself visiting one of these horrendous facilities and feeling horrified that children should be jailed in this day and age, for just being with their mum. This resulted in me becoming active in protests and ongoing work for justice and peace for folk entrapped in this inhumane system.

Confidentiality in these scenarios is of the essence, so I cannot expand on the full horror of their stories, but the experience really changed my life – and resulted in me becoming the godmother for the child involved!

Through accompanying them on their 'signing days', I got to know another Asian family. Dad was distraught, as the Home Office refused to believe his wife could not 'sign' because she was in hospital.

There followed a series of interactions with them and their two boys, where I participated in school parent-evenings and acted as an advocate for the elder boy, who had been bullied. This family introduced me to a wide network of Asian families, and whilst they have relocated to England, they remain in contact – and I was overwhelmed when they travelled north a few years back to visit me when I landed in hospital!

Another African family have two autistic children, and I accompanied mum through all their medical and educational assessments, in addition to their asylum processes, and work with her to secure their rights.

All of these families, not being allowed to take paid employment, had involved themselves in the community doing voluntary work (and whilst many locals supported them, they did have to suffer the ignorance and prejudice of a minority who were unaware of the reality of their situation).

Together we secured clothing, furniture and household goods from the streets and charity shops and shared these resources around. A barter economy evolved wherein, for instance, I offered lifts for people and to transport goods, and in return learnt to accept the multicultural food offerings, and was honoured to share with many families their often meagre rations, but more so to listen to their stories, their fears, their hopes …

This whole experience has been a real gift to me, full of joys and heartbreak – but wow. I still muse on how this auld disabled woman could get into this – and gain six African godchildren out of it, but I think my vulnerability perhaps linked with theirs; though different, we all have hearts that beat the same.

Chris Mercer

On coppiced trees

Poem from Iona Community Continentals Week 2019 in the Netherlands, the theme of which was 'the joy of creation'.

On trees, cut – and growing again,
cut – and growing again.

This patience you have is so miraculous.
Stopped, and yet you decide to start up, all again.
Bereft of leaves and fruit, and there you go, a first green leaf showing up.
Please can you spare some of this patience for me?
Please can you help this planet, cut and cut and cut,
to keep going, keep growing,
a place to live,
a tree planted with its roots reaching to the living water?

Roel Bosch

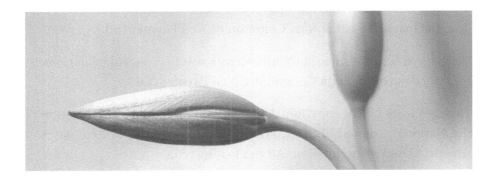

Sources and acknowledgements

'Coping', by Katharine M Preston, was first published in *Coracle*, the magazine of the Iona Community, Neil Paynter (Ed.)

'Poverty and passion: A reflection for Maundy Thursday', by Niall Cooper, from the Church Action on Poverty website: www.church-poverty.org.uk

'Road to Calvary', by Peter Phillips, was first published in *Coracle*, the magazine of the Iona Community, Neil Paynter (Ed.)

'Why?', by Brian Quail, from the Trident Ploughshares website: http://tridentploughshares.org/defence-of-brian-quail/

'This poem changes nothing', by Niall Cooper, was first published in *e-Coracle*, Neil Paynter (Ed.): www.iona.org.uk

'Healed within', by Peter Millar, from *Pipeline*, the newsletter of the Wellspring Community in Australia: https://wellspring-community.com

'Hanging out with friends', by Martin Johnstone, was first published in *Coracle*, the magazine of the Iona Community, Neil Paynter (Ed.)

'Hearts that beat the same', by Chris Mercer, was first published in *Coracle*, the magazine of the Iona Community, Neil Paynter (Ed.)

Passages from NRSV copyright 1989, Division of Christian Education of the National Council of the Churches of Christ in the United States of America. Used by permission. All rights reserved.

Good News Bible © 1994 published by the Bible Societies/HarperCollins Publishers Ltd UK, Good News Bible© American Bible Society 1966, 1971, 1976, 1992. Used with permission.

About the contributors

Rodney Aist is a pilgrim scholar and Methodist minister. He has served Christian communities in Scotland, Jerusalem, Italy and the United States.

Tim Aldred is an associate member of the Iona Community. He lives with his family in Bromley, Kent and works for the Fairtrade Foundation.

Warren Bardsley is a retired minister living in Lichfield; has served as a human rights observer in Jerusalem and the West Bank with the WCC Ecumenical Accompaniment Programme, and has written three books on the Palestinian struggle for justice and human rights. He is one of the founder members of the Kairos Britain movement.

Roel Bosch is a minister in Zeist, a parish of the Protestantse Kerk Nederland. He is an associate of the Iona Community, and translated *A Wee Worship Book: 5th Incarnation* into Dutch. He is a volunteer in woods and fields, with a special interest in reading the landscape.

Anna Briggs is a member of the Iona Community.

Ruth Burgess is a member of the Iona Community living in Dunblane. She enjoys being retired, gardening, writing and editing. When she gets the chance she likes paddling along the beach.

Alex Clare-Young is an Iona Community member and URC minister. As a transmasculine person, Alex is particularly passionate about ministering with the transgender community.

Nancy Cocks is a retired Canadian Presbyterian minister who has served at the MacLeod Centre on Iona. An associate of the Iona Community, she dedicates time to developing all-age liturgies and working with refugees settling into her community.

Niall Cooper is the Director of Church Action on Poverty and an associate of the Iona Community.

Sarah Dickinson is an elder in the Church of Scotland and author of *While Swans Fly and Herons Wait* (Bramdean Press). Between 2004 and 2019, Sarah led contemplative prayer groups and retreats, for which she regularly wrote reflections.

Judy Dinnen is an associate of the Iona Community and loves the island, the waves, rocks and the colours of the sky, but glad now to belong to a local Iona Community Family Group! She leads poetry retreats and workshops, enjoying the marriage of word and spirituality.

Carol Dixon was born in Alnwick, Northumberland and is a lay preacher in the United Reformed Church and a Friend of St Cuthbert's, Lindisfarne, for whom she produced a CD of Holy Island hymns. Her prayers and hymns are in HymnQuest, the URC Prayer Handbook and the Church of Scotland hymnbook (CH4) and she also writes for the international Christian blog godspacelight.com. She is a wife, mother and grandmother and enjoys touring with her husband in their caravette.

Donald Eadie is a former Chairman of the Birmingham District of the Methodist Church, who retired early following three spinal operations, and discovered new companions in the 'borderlands'. Through marriage, Sweden is his second home. He is the author of *Into the Foothills of Transformation* (Wild Goose).

Brian Ford: 'I am a retired sixth form college teacher. Besides writing poetry I enjoy gardening, amateur dramatics (particularly Shakespeare and pantomime) and folk music.'

Kathy Galloway is a member of the Iona Community, and currently one of its co-Leaders. She is a writer and theologian, and lives in Glasgow.

Elaine Gisbourne lives in North Yorkshire, works as a Palliative Care Physiotherapist in a hospice, and is a Spiritual Director. Her writing is often inspired by the stories and people she encounters through her work and life.

Laura Gisbourne: 'I'm a founding member of the new Iona Community youth group, earn a living as a baker in Lancashire, and spend my free time practising yoga, as an amateur actress, and dancing round my room.'

Allan Gordon is a retired consultant obstetrician and gynaecologist. He has been a member of the Iona Community for 48 years, and the members' Rule about committing time for regular engagement with the Bible and other material which nourishes has always been a most meaningful priority for him.

Timothy Gorringe taught theology in India, Oxford, St Andrews and Exeter. He is ordained and helps in the local team ministry as well as running a smallholding with his wife, Gill. His most recent book is *The World Made Otherwise* (Cascade, 2018).

Martin Johnstone is involved in a number of different organisations supporting people to speak out against poverty and injustice, both in Scotland and further afield. He is an associate member of the Iona Community.

Janet Killeen, retired from teaching, is involved with the community of her church, St George's, in South London. She writes poetry and short stories, including the collection *Recognition*, and her first novel, *After the Flood*, which will be followed in 2020 by its sequel, *Release the Raven*.

Janet Lees is a writer and a Lay Benedictine. In 2019 she walked the 'End to End' supported by her husband Bob (who walked it in 2003) and her daughter Hannah (who walked it in 2012). She is the author of *Word of Mouth* and *Tell Me the Stories of Jesus* (Wild Goose), which are both about using the remembered Bible.

Christian MacLean is a co-Leader of the Iona Community.

Rebeka Maples is Director of Spiritual Formation for the United Methodist Church programme Course of Study School of Ohio at Methodist Theological School in Ohio. She retired from parish ministry, after serving churches in England and the U.S. Her inspiration comes from nature, the arts and running half-marathons, with an eye for the holy wherever it may appear. She is a member of Spiritual Directors International and an associate member of the Iona Community.

Stephen J Maunder is a Methodist presbyter currently in ministry in Oxford. He has previously produced liturgies for Maundy Thursday and Good Friday for Wild Goose.

John McCall, an associate member of the Iona Community, has been teaching at seminaries in Taiwan for over twenty years. He also mentors, accompanies and learns from pastors throughout Asia.

Tony McClelland is a Methodist minister in Birmingham, now retired through ill health. His poems usually emerge in the cold hours when the struggle to breathe is both a question and a prayer.

Alastair McIntosh is the author of *Soil and Soul: People versus Corporate Power* (Aurum) and *Poacher's Pilgrimage: An Island Journey* (Birlinn). He lives in Govan, where he is a trustee of the GalGael Trust and an honorary professor at Glasgow University.

Chris Mercer is a 69-year-old member of the Iona Community, having joined in 1976, at the same time as joining the Catholic Church, which has made her more ecumenical as the years have gone on. She is a disabled person, having been forced to retire for medical reasons in her 30s following serious assault injuries in a domestic incident, which decimated her career as a social worker, but has led to a lifetime of active voluntary work.

Peter Millar is a theologian, activist and writer who has worked in many parts of the world, including in the Church of South India with his late wife, Dorothy. He is a former Warden of Iona Abbey and the author of several books relating the Christian faith to the hopes and struggles of our world today. Since 2016 Peter has been living with myeloma, an incurable but treatable cancer.

Susan Miller is a locum minister in the Church of Scotland at St James Church, Pollok. She also teaches courses in New Testament at Glasgow University, and has published *Women in Mark's Gospel* (Continuum).

Neil Paynter is an editor, writer and late-night piano player, who lives with his partner Helen, his mum and Stevie the cat in a flat in Biggar, Scotland.

Previously he worked in nursing homes and homeless shelters in the UK and Canada.

Peter Phillips is an associate member of the Iona Community.

Benjamin Pratt is a retired United Methodist pastor, a pastoral counsellor and the author of *A Guide for Caregivers* and *Short Stuff from a Tall Guy* (Read the Spirit). Benjamin and his wife, Judith, live in a continuing care community in Ashburn, Virginia, USA.

Katharine M Preston is an ecumenical lay preacher and writer, concentrating on issues of social justice and climate change (*Field with a View*, Wild Goose). She and her husband, John Bingham, live on a farm in Essex, New York and are active associates of the Iona Community.

Brian Quail: Prisoner No. 133799 Quail, Brian Michael, religion R.C., born 24/03/1938, former Principal Teacher Latin Greek Russian, father of seven, grandfather to fifteen, member Pax Christi, Iona Community, Scottish CND, SCANA, Catholic Worker, Trident Ploughshares, into Russian icons, wildflowers, Bach, curry, reggae, Gaelic, Ravi Shankar, poetry, Gregorian plainchant, beer, history, Orthodoxy, the Georgian language, the Shroud of Turin, Russian Church music, Bob Marley, daffodils, dancing, Dostoyevsky and Mozart.

Thom M Shuman, an associate member of the Iona Community, is a retired pastor, though still serving a church. He hopes his daily writings here offer words of hope, peace, justice and inclusion to an increasingly divided world. He is the author of *Grace Will Walk Us Home* (Wild Goose).

Richard Skinner: Richard is a poet, with several collections to his name, and a writer/performer of comedy. A Londoner by birth, he lives in Exeter where he is a member of the city centre parish.

Jan Sutch Pickard, an Iona Community member, poet and storyteller, was Warden of Iona Abbey earlier this century. After serving twice as an Ecumenical Accompanier in the West Bank Palestinian Territories, she returned to live in the west of Mull, where she continues to write and preaches in the village churches.

Reinhild Traitler-Espiritu is an educator and theologian, long-time director of the Boldern Protestant Academy (Zurich) and a former staff member of the World Council of Churches. Presently she serves as a member of the Swiss Interreligious Thinktank and as honorary president of the European Project for Interreligious Learning (EPIL). Among her many publications are two books of poetry (in German).

Iain Whyte is a retired minister and University Chaplain who has been a member of the Iona Community since 1966. He has campaigned and written on issues in Africa and Palestine, as well as historical and contemporary slavery.

Isabel Whyte is a member of the Iona Community, who first went to an Iona Youth Camp in 1961, then later to cook and lead. She has been a teacher and Healthcare Chaplain and has had a lifelong involvement in peacemaking and issues of justice.

Brian Woodcock is a retired United Reformed Church minister. He is a member of the Iona Community and was Warden of Iona Abbey from 1998 to 2001.

Martin Wroe is a writer living in London. With Malcolm Doney he is the author of *Lifelines: Notes on Life & Love, Faith & Doubt* (Unbound).

Wild Goose Publications is part of the Iona Community:

- An ecumenical movement of people from different walks of life and different traditions in the Christian church
- Committed to the gospel of Jesus Christ, and to following where that leads, even into the unknown
- Engaged together, and with people of goodwill across the world, in acting, reflecting and praying for justice, peace and the integrity of creation
- Convinced that the inclusive community we seek must be embodied in the community we practise

Together with our staff, we are responsible for:

- Our islands residential centres of Iona Abbey, the MacLeod Centre on Iona, and Camas Adventure Centre on the Ross of Mull

and in Glasgow:

- The administration of the Community
- Our work with young people
- Our publishing house, Wild Goose Publications
- Our association in the revitalising of worship with the Wild Goose Resource Group

www.ionabooks.com

The Iona Community was founded in Glasgow in 1938 by George MacLeod, minister, visionary and prophetic witness for peace, in the context of the poverty and despair of the Depression. Its original task of rebuilding the monastic ruins of Iona Abbey became a sign of hopeful rebuilding of community in Scotland and beyond. Today, we are about 280 Members, mostly in Britain, and 1500 Associate Members, with 1400 Friends worldwide. Together and apart, 'we follow the light we have, and pray for more light'.

For information on the Iona Community contact:
The Iona Community, 21 Carlton Court,
Glasgow G5 9JP, UK. Phone: 0141 429 7281
e-mail: admin@iona.org.uk; web: www.iona.org.uk

For enquiries about visiting Iona, please contact:
Iona Abbey, Isle of Iona, Argyll PA76 6SN, UK. Phone: 01681 700404
e-mail: enquiries@iona.org.uk

Wild Goose Publications, the publishing house of the Iona Community established in the Celtic Christian tradition of Saint Columba, produces books, e-books, CDs and digital downloads on:

- holistic spirituality
- social justice
- political and peace issues
- healing
- innovative approaches to worship
- song in worship, including the work of the Wild Goose Resource Group
- material for meditation and reflection

For more information:

Wild Goose Publications
The Iona Community
21 Carlton Court, Glasgow, G5 9JP, UK

Tel. +44 (0)141 429 7281
e-mail: admin@ionabooks.com

or visit our website at
www.ionabooks.com
for details of all our products and online sales